MENTAL ILLNESS

MENTAL ILLNESS

by Gilda Berger

FRANKLIN WATTS
New York/London/Toronto/Sydney/1981

Library of Congress Cataloging in Publication Data
Berger, Gilda.
Mental illness.

Bibliography: p.
Includes index.
Summary: Describes symptoms of mental illness,
treatments, and legal rights of mental patients.
1. Psychology, Pathological—Juvenile literature.   2. Psychotherapy—Juvenile literature.
3. Mental health services—United States—Juvenile
literature.   [1. Mental illness.   2. Psychotherapy]
I. Title.
RC454.4.B48   616.89   81-3059
ISBN 0-531-04343-6   AACR2

Contents

1

Changing Views Through History

I

2

Who Are the Mentally Ill?

9

3

The Neuroses

25

4

The Psychoses

35

5

Other Mental Illnesses

51

6

Treating Mental Illness

57

7

Aftercare and Rehabilitation

73

8
Rights of Mental Patients
85

Appendix 1.
Bibliography
103

Appendix 2.
Suggested Reading
107

Appendix 3.
Supplementary Tables
110

Appendix 4.
For Further Information or Professional Help
115

Appendix 5.
Advocacy and Self-Help Groups
119

Appendix 6.
Publications by
Ex-Patient Organizations
123

Appendix 7.
Glossary
125

Index
133

MENTAL ILLNESS

1

Changing Views
Through History

From 500,000 years ago right through to today, people have cast about for ways to deal with those in their families or communities who show disturbing behaviors. There has been some progress over the years in the care and treatment of mental illness, especially in the last century, but a few very important questions still remain:

• What is the root cause of mental illness? Is it a disorder of the mind, of the body, or of some interaction between mind and body?
• What are the different kinds of mental illness? What are neuroses? psychoses?
• How should mental illness be treated? With psychological therapies? drugs? supernutrition? electroshock? surgery? or combined treatments?
• Who should care for the mentally ill? The family? local communities? large state institutions? local mental health centers? halfway houses? self-help groups?

Views on mental illness keep changing. Perhaps the best way to understand the present situation is to take a backward glance over the long history of treatment from the Stone Age to the Space Age.

Shunned and Punished

Fossil remains of human bones from prehistoric times seem to show that medicine men treated those judged to be mentally ill by cutting circular openings in their skulls. Presumably, this was to release the evil spirits that were causing the problem. From observing primitive tribes living in our own time, scientists assume that there were also religious rites, such as fasting, flogging, and noisemaking, to drive the evil spirits out of the body.

The belief that deviant, or strange, behavior is caused by outside spirits taking over the body was held throughout most of human history. The Eber Papyrus of ancient Egypt says, ". . . his mind raves through something entering from above." And among the early Greeks, there was the popular saying, "Whom the gods destroy, they first make mad." Widely told myths, such as the one about the goddess Hera driving Hercules insane, leading him to burn his house and kill his wife and children, reinforced this idea.

In early civilizations, the family and local community cared for those who exhibited deviant behavior. A notable exception in both the care and treatment of the mentally ill was provided in ancient Greece around the fifth and fourth centuries B.C. by the physician Hippocrates (460–377 B.C.). First, public care was offered in so-called "healing temples." And Hippocrates was the first physician to say that mental illness, as well as other illnesses, stemmed from natural, not supernatural, causes. "For my part," he wrote, "I do not believe that the human body is ever befouled by a god." He kept thorough records on his mental patients and insisted that the patients be carefully observed and well treated.

The Hippocratic tradition of treating people with mental illness the same as other sick people continued through the period of Roman rule. Ancient Romans used public funds to treat their sick from about the fourth century B.C. until the death of the physician Galen in A.D. 200. But as Roman civilization declined, so did the pursuit of science and the practice of medicine.

During the Middle Ages, from about A.D. 400 until the mid-1400s, there was a return to superstition, fear, and ignorance in regard to mental illness. Great social unrest, devastating wars, and fearsome plagues made people's lives miserable. Many projected their unhappiness and fears onto those considered deviant. In a throwback to primitive beliefs, the mentally ill were considered to be possessed by the devil. Scholars, religious leaders, even physicians, considered it their sacred duty to cast out the devil from "mad" people. Treatment involved prayers to God, insults and curses on the demon, and eventually torture of the hapless victims.

Because the mentally ill were identified with the devil, many were accused of being witches. Most often these "witches," perhaps unusual in some behavior or strange in appearance, were older women. Writings of the time, though, described witches as an organized sect in the service of the devil, bent on disturbing the social order and destroying the faith. They were blamed for storms, floods, fires, and other catastrophes. The accused were tortured until they "confessed." Then, to save their souls, they were sentenced to death by hanging or burning at the stake. Tens of thousands of innocent people died this way in Europe through the late fifteenth century.

The mentally ill who were not tortured or killed were shunned and banned from living in the towns. Many were forced to roam the countryside. Some were packed into "ships of fools" and sent from port to port, before they were abandoned or left to die at sea.

Many of the European myths on mental illness were brought to America by the colonists in the sixteenth and early seventeenth centuries. Belief in devils and sorcery was widespread, and those believed to be witches were jailed, put in stocks, beaten at whipping posts, or hanged.

Fanaticism reached its climax in Massachusetts with the

Salem witchcraft trials of 1692 and 1693. By the time the trials ended, religious and scientific thinking about the mentally ill was beginning to change. A more secular society viewed the mentally ill as people who were sick rather than possessed. But society was still afraid of them. It was still believed that they were dangerous and that society had to be protected from them. From this came the idea of locking up those thought to be mentally ill.

Locked Up

One of the first and perhaps the most notorious of all mental institutions, Bethlehem Hospital was opened in London in 1547. Although founded on high principles, it soon became infamous as a wild, crowded, noisy, filthy place. Bedlam, the popular nickname for Bethlehem Hospital, is a word that has come to mean chaos and confusion.

Patients at Bedlam were chained and beaten. Those who were violent or outrageous in their behavior were put on public display for a penny a look. Others were sent out to wander the streets during the day as beggars.

Monasteries throughout the British Isles and Europe that had been abandoned as a result of the Reformation were adapted as places of confinement for the mentally ill. Patients were underfed and left with little or no clothing in dark, cold, unsanitary cells.

With the coming of the Industrial Revolution, there was a shift of population from small towns to larger cities. More and more people now looked outside the family or local community for care of the mentally disturbed. The emerging ethic on the virtue of hard work and frugality led to new policies on how to deal with "noncontributing" members of society.

More communities set up asylums and other institutions to isolate these burdensome individuals. Within these awful places people were sometimes shackled to the walls by hoops around the waist and iron collars. Those who were violent or who rebelled against their imprisonment were bled to weaken their resistance and make them easy to control. In the name of treatment, patients were starved, forced to take cold baths, hung by straps from the ceiling, spun around in whirling chairs, or made to suffer in various other ways.

Humane Treatment

A reaction against these inhuman conditions was slowly brought about by the new spirit of humanism that led to the French Revolution and the Age of Enlightenment. In 1756 Benjamin Franklin opened the Pennsylvania Hospital in Philadelphia, with facilities for the care of the mentally ill. Seventeen years later, the first institution in America devoted just to the care of mental patients was opened in Williamsburg, Virginia. Over the next fifty years, various private organizations and government bodies opened new institutions to house and treat mental patients.

These advances grew, in part, from the compassionate practices of France's Philippe Pinel (1745–1826) and England's William Tuke (1732–1822). Pinel's "moral treatment" of mental hospital patients in Paris proved that kindness and humane treatment accomplished more than the older harsh treatments. Tuke's well-run treatment center, located in a country setting in York, England, achieved good results in the patients and helped change attitudes toward mental illness. In America Dr. Benjamin Rush (1745–1813) spread the view of mental disorders as illnesses that were curable by kinder methods, therapy, exercise, and clean living quarters for patients. But because knowledge on the causes and treatment of mental illness was so scanty, the use of mechanical restraints, bleeding, and cold baths persisted and were used even by Rush himself.

By the last half of the nineteenth century, though, overcrowding and other abominable conditions plagued mental hospitals once more. Dorothea Lynde Dix (1802–1887), the "lone-eagle moral reformer," crusaded for more humane treatment of the mentally ill. To this end, a number of special state institutions were built, and Dix succeeded in founding or enlarging many mental hospitals throughout the country. But mentally ill inmates were still considered less than human, and hospitals remained places of confinement, not treatment.

Twentieth-Century Advances

The first part of the twentieth century saw the continued growth of more humanized attitudes toward the mentally ill. One of the most important contributions to this view was the revolutionary work of Sigmund Freud (1856–1939) in the late nineteenth and early twentieth centuries.

Freud set out to explain what lay behind the symptoms of mental illness. He focused attention on the struggles of each of us to resolve inner conflicts between the various parts of our personality. According to Freud, people who resolve this struggle live more normal lives. Individuals who do not, who have unresolved conflicts, show the symptoms of emotional disorders. Further, said Freud, the patient can often get rid of the symptoms by gaining insights into the reasons behind the difficulties. Not only did Freud's work offer a rational, logical explanation of mental illness, but it also offered hope for treating and curing the condition.

Publication of Clifford Beers' book, *A Mind That Found Itself* (1908), also helped to better the situation. In the book, Beers tells about the harsh treatment and unpleasant conditions he experienced as a patient in various mental institutions and how he finally recovered in the home of an attendant who befriended him. Beers wanted to correct the public's attitudes toward the mentally ill. As a result of his efforts, the National Committee for Mental Hygiene was formed and went to work to improve mental institutions and to foster better care and treatment for all patients with mental disorders.

The interest in the mentally ill grew considerably during the 1940s, the years of World War II. Three of every five men, it was learned, were unfit for military service because of mental or emotional disorders. And then, among those who were accepted and who saw combat, there was a widespread condition known as "battle fatigue." The symptoms of this illness included sleeplessness, frequent nightmares, anxiety, tremors, and loss of appetite. Both factors inspired scores of different institutions, from the armed services to universities and hospitals, to undertake research into the causes and treatment of mental illness.

During the 1950s tranquilizing drugs were introduced as a treatment for mental illness. Many who had been written off as hopeless cases were now dramatically relieved of their disturbing symptoms and were able to live more normal lives. As a result, laws were passed authorizing the discharge from hospitals of patients who would be able to receive outpatient treatment in the community and could continue at a job or school while living at home.

Research into the relationship of body chemistry and mental illness has led to new medications and special diets that are achieving successful results in some patients. Alternate approaches to therapy, including greater use of group therapy, also show great promise. Preventive care, through education and counseling, is making a valuable contribution. Most experts now recognize that many different factors contribute to the cause of mental illness, and that all therapies need to be considered in treatment.

The View Ahead

In spite of improved attitudes and advances in research, there are still many problems for those whom we call mentally ill.

While drugs relieve the symptoms of many disorders and enable many patients to return to the outside world, they are certainly not the hoped-for cure-alls. A significant number of patients who are discharged on maintenance doses return again and again to hospitals. Many others suffer permanently harmful side effects that are sometimes even more distressing than their original disorders.

Deinstitutionalized patients often encounter difficulties getting along in the community. Some find it hard to locate housing, get jobs, and obtain credit. Many are abandoned in rooming houses, dilapidated hotels, or even on city streets because of insufficient funding or facilities. Some return to hospitals simply because they have nowhere else to go.

Thousands with mental or emotional problems are still without proper care or treatment. The aged, especially women, are frequently hospitalized unnecessarily for mental illness. Many of the severely retarded are housed in mental institutions where little attempt is made to improve their functioning.

Conditions in some mental hospitals are still far from good. There is evidence of gross physical abuse by some attendants and incorrect use of drugs on certain types of patients. In Florida, a four-month investigation found evidence of the sexual abuse of some patients, overuse of drugs, and medical neglect. Many patients' rooms were filthy or infested with fleas, rats, or roaches.

The contemporary chapter in the history of mental illness is being written today by us. What will future accounts say about *our* attitudes and about *our* efforts in the care and treatment of the mentally ill?

2

Who Are the Mentally Ill?

The mentally ill are people who find it hard or impossible to deal with the ordinary stresses of daily life because of disorders or disturbances of the mind or body. The youngster who doesn't have any friends, the man who has a hacking cough without an apparent physical cause, the gifted young man who says he wants to commit suicide, the elderly woman who cannot remember where she lives—such people may be suffering from mental illness.

Some say the mentally ill are people whose needs or problems differ only in degree from those of others. In other words, most people get depressed at times, but severe, long-lasting depression can be a sign of mental illness. Others believe that severe mental disorders are diseases, just like heart disease or cancer. They say that the deviant behaviors are the outward symptoms of the sickness.

Everyone agrees, though, that there are many different forms of mental illness. The behavior of some sufferers is only slightly different from what is considered normal. For others it is much greater. In some cases the signs of disturbance appear only occasionally. A few show bizarre behavior that is present all the time.

Generally speaking, then, the term "mentally ill" is used to refer to people with a whole range of mental or emotional

problems. This includes those whose lives are unhappy or difficult but who get along day to day and those who have distorted views of reality and cannot function in the world without special care and treatment.

What Causes Mental Illness?

At present there are at least three widely accepted theories on
the cause of mental illness.

The longest-held view, the so-called organic model, is
that all mental disorders stem from physical changes in or
damage to the body. For example, certain disorders are known
to be related to brain damage that occurs before, during, or
right after birth, or as the result of a stroke later in life. Problems may develop because of a serious infection such as syphilis or encephalitis. A tumor, or growth, on the brain may also
bring about personality changes. Some deficiency conditions,
such as pellagra, have been found to interfere with the functioning of the mind. And excessive use of drugs or alcohol or
a hard blow to the head may sometimes lead to a temporary
or permanent disturbance.

Some of the most exciting research in the field of mental
illness is now being pursued by researchers who follow the
organic model of causation. They are studying possible biochemical factors that might be related to mental illness. Their
experiments are designed to discover whether there are differ-
ences in the amounts of certain chemicals found within the
brain or nerve cells of people considered normal and those
regarded as mentally ill. Other scientists are looking to hereditary or genetic influences as possible causes. For example: Is
there a common pattern of mental illness in parents or other
relatives of the mentally ill? Are there any abnormalities in the
genetic material that can be associated with the later appearance of mental disorder?

While the idea that mental disorder has an organic base

is winning much support today, physical causes alone are not likely to be the whole answer to this difficult question. Environment surely plays a part at least some of the time. Many diseases progress in certain ways only because of the way the individual responds to the environment.

The influence of the family and surroundings on the individual is stressed in the most widely held concept, the psychosocial model of mental illness. Most emotional disturbances, by this view, are the result of poor or damaging experiences early in life, and mental illness is a learned set of behaviors growing out of a person's difficulties in dealing with society.

Youngsters with parents who are always tense or apprehensive may come to regard the world as a frightening place, with potential hazards lurking around every corner. Neglect or rejection during the first year or two of life can leave a person feeling insecure and fearful and unable to cope with difficulties. The child who runs away from problems by pretending to be sick and finds that it helps him or her to cope may grow up with this and other inappropriate ways of dealing with life situations.

The latest entry is the societal-reaction model. Advocates of this model say that deviant behaviors are not symptoms of mental illness at all. Rather they are individual ways of handling the very considerable pressures and problems of modern-day life. The psychiatrist Thomas Szasz and others say that deviant behavior is not sickness. It is merely behavior that does not happen to conform to the accepted norms of the society. Hence, they blame contemporary society for its mistaken beliefs and persecution of the mentally deviant. Present attitudes in regard to mental illness, they hold, are as outrageous in our time as were the old beliefs in evil spirits and witches.

The British psychiatrist R. D. Laing has an outlook that is somewhat similar to this view. "What we call normal," he writes, "is a product of repression, denial, splitting, projection, introjection, and other forms of destructive action or experience." In other words, normal people are not really normal; they are ill. It is those who are considered mentally ill, who do not repress or deny or hide their conflicts from others, who are closer to normal.

Experts have been disagreeing about the causes of mental illness since the beginning of history. So the fact that there are so many different views today on the causes of mental illness is certainly not new. What is new is the possibility that the cause may turn out to be a combination of causes—in the mind, in the body, and in the environment.

Prevention

Only a few mental illnesses, those resulting from particular diseases, injuries to the brain, food deficiencies, or poisons, are preventable. Unfortunately, most mental disorders are not. Someday, as researchers shed more light on the basic causes of mental illness, we may have better success with prevention. But for now, the best way to prevent most kinds of mental illness seems to be to promote mental health.

The National Association for Mental Health gives three general characteristics of people who display good mental health: they feel comfortable about themselves, they feel right about other people, and they are able to meet the demands of life.

Tom is an example of someone who feels good about himself and is able to take life's disappointments in stride. For a long time Tom was the best player on his high school football team, and he expected to win a football scholarship to the state university. He needed the scholarship since his parents could not afford to pay for his college education. Then, suddenly, Tom learned that the university was no longer awarding any scholarships.

Bitterly disappointed, Tom was unsure of what to do

next. After a few days, though, he sized up the situation and decided on a new course of action. He took a part-time job right away and started to plan for a full-time summer position. In this way, he figured, he would be able to make ends meet, even without the scholarship.

Of course, Tom felt angry and let down when he discovered he was not going to get the scholarship. But he accepted the loss and found new ways to cope with the problem.

The way we feel about ourselves, about what we are, and about what we do is not a matter of chance. It depends on many factors in both our heredity and our environment. Certain basic characteristics are inherited from our parents and grandparents and are present at birth. They even show up in newborns; one infant is calm and relaxed, while another is alert and active.

For thirty-four years, two doctors kept track of the physical and mental health of 1,337 subjects, starting when they were medical students at Johns Hopkins University. Their findings seem to show that personality has a biological basis. Factors within the body, for example, made some of the subjects more vulnerable to stress than others. Their conclusion was that the best way to maintain good mental and physical health is to accept what you are.

But we all grow up in environments that influence and shape our personal characteristics and patterns of behavior. The way we are regarded at home influences our personality development. The way our parents and other siblings show love and affection, discipline and protection, helps us to form our self-image. Often, the way the family members see us becomes the model on which we pattern our behavior.

In spite of the effects of our heredity and environment, we can learn to adapt and modify our own behavior and lifestyle. Behavior, at least to some extent, is under our conscious control. It is, though, strongly influenced by past experiences and how we reacted to particular situations early in life.

Some years ago a study was done in California on people's attitudes and beliefs regarding mental health. The results showed that self-image is important to how people rate their own mental well-being. Those with the best self-concept said that they were in better mental health than did those who were low in self-esteem.

When we feel right about others we are able to give and receive love and to form satisfying and lasting relationships. Those who are considerate of the needs and interests of others feel a deep sense of responsibility for their fellow human beings. They like and trust others and expect the same in return. They are able to feel part of a group without losing their own identity.

One day Sally's boyfriend told her that he wanted to break up their relationship and date other girls. For a while Sally was very blue. But after talking to her friends and family, she realized it was all for the best. She adjusted to her new situation by accepting dates with other boys and by forming new friendships. As a result, she got to know some boys whom she liked even better than her old boyfriend.

Sally's healthy feelings about herself in relation to others helped her find her way. Contact with others is vital for good mental health. Just as the body needs food, water, and air to function properly, so everyone needs love and affection, to be with other people, and to achieve something worthwhile, in order to function properly psychologically. This does not mean giving in to every demand that people make on us to try to win their affection or insisting on having our own way all the time. It does mean approaching others openly, making it easier for them to respond in kind, and a willingness to engage in the give and take that is part of all successful human encounters.

The same California survey cited earlier showed that low regard for other people is associated with lower levels of perceived mental health. Those who do not think highly of others, it seems, also tend to have a poor self-image. Incidentally, those same people were often found to be excessive users of alcohol and drugs.

Individuals who are best able to meet the demands of life are usually those who are active rather than merely reactive. That is, they believe in doing something about their problems, in thinking for themselves, and in making their own decisions. They work hard to succeed and enjoy the process. Their goals are realistic.

After his mother's death, fourteen-year-old Mike was overwhelmed by feelings of helplessness. He lost interest in everyone and everything and even stopped going to school.

As the days went by, Mike began to accept his loss and to realize that life had to continue. Slowly he picked up his former interests, even though thoughts about his mother were never far from his mind. Whenever he felt low he went for long bike rides or practiced the piano—the hobbies that he enjoyed most. He also returned to school and studied especially hard. As he became busy, the pain of losing his mother slowly abated.

As people mature they learn ways to handle situations that cause tension and anxiety, no matter whether the crisis is a real one, such as the death of a loved one, or an imagined one, such as the fear of an attack by an animal. When faced with stressful situations, we can respond either by getting scared and running away from the problem or by approaching it head-on and working to overcome it.

Each time we deal with stress and find that we can confront and conquer the difficulty, it becomes easier to handle the next crisis. Such experiences change our behavior. These changes, called adaptations, are important because they help us to function better. They gear the body for greater effort and protect it from harm. They are the way we meet outside threats and provide for our safety, well-being, and happiness.

A Harvard University study measured 188 graduates according to such mental health factors as job satisfaction, happiness in marriage, use of tranquilizers, and visits to psychiatrists. Those who seemed psychologically fit remained well physically. The chronic sufferers of anxiety and depression were more likely to develop physical illnesses. The lesson here might be that stress is a potential killer and that coping with stress contributes to good physical as well as mental health.

In one experiment, laboratory animals were given mild electric shocks when they were very young. When these animals grew up they tended to have better emotional reactions in coping with stress than animals who had not received the shocks. They actually became bigger and stronger adults and lived longer. In the same way, when people learn to adapt to stress, their capacity to deal with difficult situations is better. Successful coping, or so it is believed, builds greater personal strength.

A Widespread Problem

According to the Mental Health Association about 32 million people in the United States, an estimated 15 percent of the population, have emotional problems serious enough to need mental health care. Altogether, as many as 53 million people, or 25 percent of the population, show some of the symptoms of emotional disturbance. And each year, reports the association, more people enter hospitals for the treatment of mental disorders than for any other single illness. (See Table 1.)

Surveys show that about 2 million Americans are believed to be schizophrenic. People with schizophrenia, one of the most disturbing mental conditions, show symptoms that include bizarre behavior, delusions, and hallucinations. At least 2 million others suffer profound depression or severe disturbances in mood. And more than 1 million Americans have other types of permanently disabling mental conditions.

About 5.8 million people, or 25 percent of all people

Table 1.

Impact of Major Illness

	WHAT RANKS AS NUMBER 1	HOW MENTAL DISORDERS RANK
Hospital Admissions	Mental Disorders	1
Social Security Benefits Eligibility	Diseases of the Circulatory System	3
Physician Visits	Diseases of the Respiratory System	9
Limitation of Major Activities	Other Illnesses	9
Lost Work Days	Diseases of the Respiratory System	10
Confined in Bed at Home	Diseases of the Respiratory System	11
Years Lost due to Premature Death	Diseases of the Circulatory System	12

Source: Mental Health Association, rev. 1979.

over sixty-five years of age, have significant mental health problems. They make up a disproportionately large number of people in mental hospitals and other mental health facilities. Some 20 to 30 percent of those labeled as senile, however, are believed to suffer from other conditions, which might have been prevented if they had received early treatment. The elderly, although they make up only 11 percent of the population, account for 25 percent of all reported suicides.

As high as the figures on mental illness are, all signs seem to indicate that they are climbing even higher. (See Table 2.) The number of people who need or who are looking for mental health care every year is growing. Opinion is divided as to whether this indicates a greater willingness to seek help or an increase in stress and strain in everyday life.

Two groups that have shown a particularly sharp and alarming increase in mental illness are children and young adults. Using just one indicator, the suicide rate among those between ten and twenty-five years of age, we see that it has tripled in the years since the 1950s.

Table 2.
Admissions to All Mental Health Services
by Broad Age Groups, 1971 and 1975

Number of Admissions

Age of Admissions	1971	1975	Percent Increase in Admissions, 1971–1975
Under 65	2,291,119	3,194,098	39.4
65 and Over	116,368	161,610	38.9
Total Admissions	2,407,487	3,355,708	39.4

Source: Division of Biometry and Epidemiology, NIMH, 1978.

18

The overall mental illness statistics are so high that many consider mental illness a major public health problem in our country. It is so widespread that almost every one of us will, at one time or another, have a friend, relative, or acquaintance who is affected by mental illness.

Another measure of the enormity of the problem is in terms of the cost to the nation. About $17 billion was spent on mental health care and treatment in 1979. This is an estimated 12 percent of the total cost of health care in the United States. In addition, there are indirect costs, such as missed work or time lost by troubled workers, which amounts to another $20 billion.

Specialists in Mental Disorders

Because of the growing numbers of people with mental disorders, there is an increased need for professionals who can provide the help, care, and treatment required. Professionals in the field today are identified by a bewildering number of titles. Most, though, have a specific meaning.

Psychiatrists are medical doctors who specialize in the treatment of mental illnesses. They receive the same medical training as other M.D.'s, but in addition have four years of advanced training in the study, diagnosis, and treatment of a whole range of mental illnesses, from mild to severe. A psychiatrist is the only mental health professional who has a license to practice medicine and, therefore, the only one who can prescribe drugs or other medical treatments.

Psychoanalysts are psychiatrists who hold certificates that show they have been trained in the use of psychoanalysis, one of the therapies that treats patients by using conversation.

Psychiatric nurses are professional nurses who have had, beyond their regular training, advanced studies in the prevention, treatment, and rehabilitation of people with mental disturbances. Often, they help individuals or groups deal with problems in sessions held in community mental health centers, clinics, hospitals, or prisons. *Psychiatric social workers* have advanced training in social work, with a specialty in psychiatry and a background in community service.

Highly trained professionals who may have academic doctorates, called doctor of philosophy degrees, but are not physicians, are called *psychologists.* Most *clinical psychologists,* who treat individuals and groups, have doctoral degrees plus two years of experience working in mental health facilities. Clinical psychologists who have special training in using psychoanalysis to treat patients are often called *lay analysts.*

The general terms *psychotherapist, therapist,* and *counselor* are all used to refer to mental health workers who treat patients. They may include those discussed above, who are well trained and highly qualified. Or they may be titles used by individuals who are neither experienced nor well grounded. The danger is that self-appointed experts may not help at all and, in fact, can worsen the patient's condition. When seeking help for yourself or someone you know, make sure that you deal with a person who has been properly trained.

Keeping Good Mental Health

Psychiatrists and psychologists offer some good advice on how we can best cope with stressful situations and maintain good mental health.

One part of coping is to talk about the things that are worrisome. Giving vent to emotions freely, without fear of disapproval, is a healthy way to release tensions. Often, bringing out in the open feelings such as guilt or embarrassment may make them less upsetting. Sometimes it also helps point the way to a solution. Realizing that you are angry and figuring out the reasons why may give you the insights you need to handle different situations.

At times, people under tension find it helps to leave the

painful problem alone for a while and "get away from it all." A simple change of pace or a refocus of energies is constructive and not necessarily running away from the problem. Any brief escape—reading a book, taking a walk—lets you return to the difficulty in a more composed way.

When crisis piles up on top of crisis and seems overwhelming, it sometimes is valuable to break the problems down to their specifics. Once you understand all the facts, it is easier to handle them. You can focus your energies on the most pressing tasks and tackle them first. After these things are taken care of, the remaining problems frequently are handled much more easily. And being active and taking the first steps frees you from the trapped feeling that can be so paralyzing.

Some people are always worried or anxious because they expect too much from themselves and never feel that they are achieving as much as they should. They try to be perfect in everything. To avoid the inevitable frustration that this leads to, it is better to concentrate your energies on those things you do well and that offer you the most satisfaction and the greatest rewards.

The same thinking applies to setting unrealistic goals for others. Trying to make others over to suit our images of them can only lead to frustration and disappointment. Remembering that all people have strengths and weaknesses can help life run more smoothly.

Helping somebody else sometimes makes it easier to handle your own worries. By making yourself available to others, you are able to put your own difficulties into perspective and break a cycle of tension and failure.

The philosophy of the Mental Health Association is based on beliefs that have sustained people since the beginning of civilization: "Faith in ourselves, faith in others, faith in our ability to improve and grow, faith in our desire and capacity to work out our problems cooperatively, and faith in the essential decency of people."

Getting Help

A recent study by the National Association of Private Psychiatric Hospitals said that "about two-thirds of all psychiatric patients show significant signs of recovery, and of these, half will never need treatment again." These are impressive figures, and many people cite them as a reason to be optimistic about the future.

Studies show that the earlier a mental disorder is treated, the better the chances for improvement. Therefore, we should all be aware of signs that might indicate emotional difficulties in the people we know and the possible need for professional help. These signs are:

—extreme tension and anxiety that cannot be linked to some specific event, such as a death, an illness, or a particularly stressful or trying situation.
—excessive isolation or depression, with little interest in activities going on in the environment.
—uncharacteristic hostility, rudeness, or violence.
—sudden changes in eating or sleeping habits, or in appearance or personal hygiene, especially if they continue for a long time.
—sudden swings in mood or behavior that are inappropriate or uncharacteristic.
—complaints about physical ailments that seem to have no organic cause.

Mental health experts suggest some ways that family and friends can help people who are troubled and some things that they should avoid doing.

It is important, they say, to show those who seem to be under a lot of stress that you are sincerely interested in their problems and are genuinely concerned about their needs and feelings. Often, people who need help the most find it hardest to discuss their personal problems, and they keep their troubles bottled up inside them. "I'd rather not talk about it," or "Maybe things will improve if I don't say anything and just hang on," are common attitudes.

A friendly and attentive approach can give those who are having difficulties the chance they need to share their concerns and to get rid of some of their tensions and anxieties. There are times when all that is needed is some understanding and sympathy. If the chief problem is something specific, such as school failure, trouble at home, money, or lack of a job, you may be able to suggest ways for the person to cope with these particular stresses.

Sometimes, though, listening is not enough. If the trouble seems severe and prolonged, you should contact one of the agencies that can offer assistance in the areas of diagnosis, evaluation, treatment, and whatever else is needed. Professionally trained staff members in community mental health centers, clinics, and hospitals are there to help people with mental, emotional, or personality problems.

If someone you know has a sudden attack of mental illness—becomes violent, goes completely out of control, or attempts to commit suicide—there are several things you should do. First, try to remain calm. For people who are currently under treatment for a mental condition, it is best to call the hospital, clinic, or therapist already involved. Failing this you should call the person's doctor or try to get the person to the nearest hospital.

Should you need an ambulance, call the police, the fire department, or the local rescue squad. You will find the emergency numbers in the front of your telephone directory. In the event of an extreme emergency—the person seems likely to seriously injure someone—dial the police emergency number, 911. You can also get help by calling the mental health hot-line, the suicide prevention center, or a drug abuse hot-line, if there are such services where you live.

There are several important "don'ts" in helping a person undergoing an episode of disorganization or emotional distress. Don't, for example, express your opinion of the person's behavior. Don't make comments such as "You're being silly," or "It's nothing to worry about." These remarks only strengthen the individual's belief that no one cares or understands and may lead to further isolation and greater anxiety.

But above all, don't advise a troubled person to "snap out of it." Usually the person is unable to do anything about the strange behavior or wild actions. Telling him or her to stop just adds to the person's already strong feelings of helplessness and despair. While many of us like to think that we can analyze the causes of disturbed behavior, it is best to seek professional help and not to attempt diagnosis or treatment on our own.

3

The Neuroses

Nearly everyone gets anxious, tense, or fearful when facing a difficult situation. It is not unusual to be worried before a first date, to have sweaty palms during a difficult exam, or to experience "butterflies in the stomach" before making a speech.

But some people seem to be extremely anxious or extremely tense nearly all the time, even when there is no apparent reason. They react with fear and dread to situations that most others do not consider either dangerous or threatening. Often they are also unhappy, suffer headaches and indigestion, have deep feelings of guilt, sometimes act in irrational ways, and go to great lengths to avoid coping with their real problems. The simplest routines of day-to-day life become difficult to handle. Such people are called *neurotics;* they are said to be suffering from *neuroses* (pl. of *neurosis*) *disorders.*

Constant Anxiety

Jane, at twenty-three years old, was an example of someone with neurotic symptoms of behavior. As a young girl, Jane dreamed of becoming a dancer on Broadway. She starred in high school and dance studio productions in her hometown in Ohio. After less than a year in college, she dropped out to try to launch a career in New York. But she did not succeed at any of the auditions she attended, and so she began working as a waitress to support herself.

Most of the time, though, Jane found herself feeling tired and depressed, without any obvious physical cause. She was very irritable and was finding it hard to hold on to her job and to keep the few friends she made. Not only did she feel tense and anxious most of the time, but her heart raced, she perspired profusely, and she felt short of breath several times every day.

Sigmund Freud once said that a neurotic is someone who is "at war with himself." Most neurotics share general patterns of behavior and feelings that prevent them from realizing their full potential. Often they feel that they are not good enough, smart enough, or talented or attractive enough to succeed in a hostile world. They are fearful and anxious about meeting new people or starting new tasks. And even when things are going well, they feel that their success will somehow lead to failure.

Typically, neurotics go through life hiding, running away, and using a variety of defenses to avoid facing and coping with their problems. Students frequently wake up feeling sick on days of important exams. One neurotic young man, for instance, always found excuses to break up any developing relationships with girl friends because he was afraid of getting married.

People with neuroses usually find it emotionally exhausting to deal with their fearful anxieties. Perhaps they are aware that they are not functioning as well as they might, but generally they cannot find the source of their anxiety. They do not recognize the elaborate cover-ups they use to protect themselves against their fears, nor are they able to control their thoughts or actions.

As a result, neurotics seem to have little time or energy

26

for living full, satisfying lives or for offering love and affection to others. The struggle with their emotions leaves some neurotics feeling defeated and with an apparent lack of joy or purpose in their lives. Neurotics can usually function and manage their affairs, but seldom as well as they would were they free of this inner turmoil.

Kinds of Neuroses

On the basis of the symptoms, all neuroses can be divided into a number of separate categories. The most common is called *anxiety neurosis*. An estimated 20 million people in the United States alone, about 30 to 40 percent of all those with neuroses, experience the mental or physical symptoms of anxiety. They feel fearful, uneasy, helpless, and nervous but not necessarily in reaction to specific threats to them as individuals.

People such as Jane, suffering from anxiety neurosis, generally feel tense and worried. Under strain or stress, they feel even worse. Also, they may suffer the symptoms of anxiety reactions long after the stressful situation that produced the original response has passed. Acute attacks of fear and dread may strike suddenly and for no apparent reason. During these episodes, which can last up to an hour, the person may have a very fast, strong heartbeat, may find it hard to breathe, and may perpsire heavily. Despite this, the skin is usually cold. On occasion, the symptoms are so severe that they are mistaken for a heart attack.

Some anxiety neurotics are confused and troubled by the way they feel. On the other hand, many blame their behavior on other people. Most cases are mild. Only a few find that they cannot function socially, cannot hold a job or attend school, or need to be hospitalized. Statistics show that anxiety neurosis does not seem to run in families, that it occurs on all socioeconomic levels, and that many more women than men are affected. One explanation for the relatively small percentage

27

of males in this category is that many men may hide their anxiety symptoms by using alcohol or by other cover-ups.

Forty-year-old Jeff has another type of neurotic disorder. One day, while standing on a ladder painting the outside of his house, Jeff suddenly felt dizzy and thought he was going to faint. He called to his wife to help him down from the ladder. The next day he wanted to finish the paint job, but as he approached the ladder his hands started perspiring and his heart pounded. He was absolutely terrified of climbing the ladder. His wife tried to convince him to go up a few rungs. He did, but froze in place on the third one. A neighbor had to be called to help him down.

Jeff's fear of heights became so paralyzing that it now takes all of his willpower just to step up on a stool to reach something from a high shelf. Even standing on the ground and looking up at a tall building can make him feel uncomfortable and a bit dizzy. Jeff is said to be suffering from a *phobia neurosis*.

A phobia neurosis is a strong and persistent fear of an object or situation that actually represents much less danger than the reaction indicates. The fear of high places (acrophobia), fear of closed places (claustrophobia), fear of animals or one specific animal (zoophobia), fear of crowds (ochlophobia), and fear of darkness (nyctophobia) are some common phobias. Altogether it is estimated that about 10 million Americans suffer from one or more phobias.

Some of the things that phobics fear scare most everyone to some extent. But the neurotic's reactions are much stronger, cause greater anguish, and last longer than those of most others. In some cases, the panic reaction is triggered by things that do not bother most people at all. Here the feeling aroused generally bears little relation to reality.

Persons with phobic neuroses will often go to great lengths to avoid the objects of their fears. Marilyn, a young homemaker, suffers from agoraphobia, a fear of open or public places. She makes sure that either her husband or her mother is able to accompany her before she goes out shopping or for a walk. Sometimes just the thought of going into a supermarket or department store can give Marilyn an anxiety attack. If she finds herself alone in a dreaded open place, she may get a headache, a pain in her stomach, feel dizzy, or get a strange sense of being out of touch with reality. Sometimes she worries that she will pass out, have a heart attack, or even lose her sanity.

Anxiety is usually part of a phobic neurosis. In some cases a generalized anxiety is replaced by a specific phobia. Freud's study of young Hans, described in his 1909 paper, "Analysis of a Phobia in a Five-Year-Old Boy," is a classic example.

Hans feared going out into the street. He said that it was because he was afraid that a horse would bite him. The fear may have been related to the fact that one day while Hans was riding in a carriage, his horse fell and was injured. Freud's analysis of the phobia was that Hans had had anxious and fearful thoughts of his father, whom the boy unconsciously felt was competing with him for his mother's love. By displacing the fear to horses (zoophobia), Hans kept his real feelings hidden and retained the love of his father. Others might say that the boy's fear of horses was simply a reaction to the unpleasant incident of the horse being injured and that Hans held on to the phobia because avoiding horses lessened his generalized anxiety.

In the play *Macbeth*, Lady Macbeth frequently rubs her hands together for several minutes at a time. As she does this she says, "Out, damned spot! Out, I say!" and makes other references to blood on her hands. The recurring behavior and thoughts represent Lady Macbeth's guilt for her part in the murder of King Duncan.

In this play Shakespeare has portrayed perfectly the particular neurosis of persons who perform actions, often inappropriately, that they do not want to perform (compulsions), or have repeated and uncontrolled thoughts (obsessions). This kind of neurosis is called *obsessive-compulsive*. The two words are linked together because obsessive and compulsive behaviors often occur in the same people. About 15 percent of those with neuroses fall into this category.

Many of us have ritual actions that we always follow, such as not stepping on cracks in the sidewalk, or repeated thoughts, such as that we are too fat or too thin. Obsessive-compulsive neurotics, though, often indulge in much more extreme behavior. There is the woman who vacuums her house several times a day or the business executive whose mind always dwells on the notion that he will die of cancer at an early age.

For obsessive-compulsive neurotics, life centers around their persistent thoughts and ritual actions. They may have guilty thoughts about murdering someone they know well, stealing a great deal of money, or even about committing suicide. Most people with obsessions and compulsions know that their ideas and behaviors are irrational. Although they find their thoughts and actions troublesome and unwelcome, too often they cannot stop them without help.

Everyone feels blue, let down, or discouraged at times. The death of a loved one, the loss of a job, or disappointment in a love affair are events that cause unhappiness in each of us. In fact, not feeling sad in such circumstances might be considered slightly odd.

The difference between normal depression and a severe *depressive neurosis* is that most people overcome ordinary sadness in time. They work through their feelings of unhappiness, alone or with the help of others, and renew their interests and activities. Those who suffer depressive neurosis, however, are generally sad, apathetic, and unresponsive to the world around them. As with other types of neuroses, depression becomes a disorder when it is strong, persistent, and interferes with normal functioning. Experts suspect that many people hide their depression by overworking, drinking, gambling, or by other behaviors that mask the problem.

Murray was fifty-two years old when he lost his job as an engineer and went into a deep depression. After about a year on unemployment insurance he found another job. But he continued to feel as miserable as he did the day he was fired. He spent his evenings alone, usually watching television. He blamed his wife and his grown children for his sadness, boredom, tiredness, and lack of interest in what was going on around him. Oftentimes he was cranky and irritable. Murray also felt that his memory was failing him and that he was incapable of making decisions. He complained to his doctor of everything from indigestion to headaches and dizziness, but the doctor could find nothing wrong. His doctor finally suggested that he see a psychiatrist, who diagnosed Murray as suffering from a depressive neurosis.

For some people, the state of depression comes and goes. Such eminent figures as Abraham Lincoln, Winston Churchill, and Sigmund Freud, among many others, are said to have suffered with depressive neurosis. They show that it is possible to be highly productive despite the disorder.

Many depressive individuals talk about suicide, and some actually make the attempt. About 75 percent of all attempted suicides are said to be made by depressive neurotics.

Theories on Causes

Opinions vary on the causes of neuroses. The psychoanalytic school, based on the thinking of Freud, believes that neuroses are symptoms of the struggle between conflicting impulses in the unconscious that usually start very early in life. Human behavior, they say, is determined by the development of the id, ego, and superego, the three parts of the personality. The id represents the basic unconscious and uncontrolled desires for pleasure and satisfaction; the ego is the part that is concerned with the reality of the situation; and the superego is the conscience or "ego ideal," mostly learned from one's parents.

Neurosis may occur, according to this scheme, when the ego cannot handle the demands of the id or cannot help the id conform to the realities of the world. Or the superego may take over to such an extent that all instincts for pleasure cause anxiety and worry.

Freud felt that every adult neurosis could be traced back either to a childhood neurosis or to some bad experience in childhood that interfered with the normal sequence of growth and development. Psychoanalytic treatment consists of helping the patients to understand and accept the conflicts or particular problems within their personalities, thus freeing them from the symptoms. There is little concern with treating or trying to control the actual patterns of neurotic behavior.

Two slightly different approaches are taken by the followers of Alfred Adler and Carl Jung. Both of these men were early disciples of Freud who broke away to move off in new directions. Adlerians believe that feelings of inferiority are the basis of most neuroses. It does not matter whether the feelings of inferiority are real or imagined. As long as there is a feeling of inferiority, they hold, one tries to make up for it, and this leads to the neurosis.

Tied up with the importance he gave to inferiority was Adler's concern with the "will to power," the drive people have to make themselves feel important and superior. When this will to power is frustrated, people struggle even harder to assert themselves, and the result is often neurotic, antisocial behavior. Since social relationships with family and friends play important roles in personality development, Adlerians suggest that treatment should consist of conversations that help the patients perform more successfully in situations that involve others and to understand difficulties in relating to other people.

To disciples of Carl Jung, the unconscious part of our personality is the racial heritage that we have inherited from our most primitive ancestors. They call this the collective unconscious. Neuroses, they believe, spring in part from attempts to solve today's problems using primitive methods. As part of the treatment, Jungians often ask patients to paint pictures, which may be used to bridge the gap between the collective unconscious and the day-to-day problems caused by the neurosis. Jungians accept Freud's views on the importance of infancy and childhood but believe that tracing all difficulties back to those early years is evading the real problem. They try to help patients face up to their present difficulties and sometimes go so far as to suggest solutions.

In contrast to the several psychoanalytic theories are the various behavioral theories. Behaviorists believe that neurotic patterns of behavior are learned, and therefore can be unlearned. Understanding the causes of neurotic habits, they claim, may not necessarily eliminate the unacceptable behavior. This newer view holds that neurotics are people who grew up without learning how to deal successfully with their conflicts and problems. They do not evaluate situations properly, and therefore tend to overreact, and this sometimes results in severe anxiety. Since this anxiety proves uncomfortable or even painful, they develop habits of neurotic behavior to get relief. These actions relieve their anxiety, but they become self-defeating because, by avoiding the basic problem, they merely reinforce the neurotic behavior.

The behaviorists who hold this viewpoint treat neurotics by first trying to find out which behaviors the patients wish to change. They then help the patients to find new and better behaviors to replace the unwanted ones. Finally, by a system of rewards and punishments, by gradually leading the patients to accept the new behavior, or by setting forth models for the patients to imitate, the behaviorists eliminate the undesirable behaviors and replace them with acceptable ones.

The humanist and existential concepts of neuroses borrow from both the psychoanalytic and behavioral theories. According to those who hold these ideas, every person wants to grow to be an emotionally healthy, fully functioning individual. The neurotics, they believe, move timidly and fearfully toward this goal because they have lost their sense of direction in life due to confusion between their own ideas and those of others. In other words, neurotic behavior is caused by the conflicts between what we think we should do and our perception of what others, such as parents, teachers, friends, and the community, think we should do.

Existentialists stress the special qualities of each person and the need for each individual to set his or her own standards in order to achieve the most complete self-realization possible. Pain and anxiety are not necessarily bad, since they are, after all, part of life. Rather they should be incorporated into one's being and turned into positive growing experiences. Treatment, according to the humanists and existentialists, should be nonjudgmental. In fact, the existentialists believe it is vital to get away from the idea of neurosis as a problem or illness.

A single answer to the question of what causes neuroses may never be found. There are at least as many explanations of the exact nature and origin of neuroses as there are types of disorders. Psychiatrists and psychologists of every school of thought, though, are now trying to learn more about the neuroses. With new information may come better treatment methods and more effective ways to help patients achieve better mental health.

4

The Psychoses

The psychoses are much more serious mental problems than the neuroses. People with neuroses generally live unhappy and difficult lives, but they are able to manage their affairs. Many sufferers with psychoses, however, lose contact with the real world. They find it impossible to hold jobs, go to school, or relate socially to others, at least until they receive help or treatment.

Strange Realities

Each person looks at the world in a particular way. It is not unusual for four people to see the same accident and each one come away with a slightly different perception of what really happened.

People diagnosed as *psychotic* also have their own points of view or perceptions of reality. The difference is that their views of the world are often strikingly different from the perception shared by most others. A person diagnosed as psychotic might see the same accident and say that it was caused by his bad thoughts, and therefore was his fault. On some level he might know that he did not cause the accident, but he is not able to control his reactions.

People who break with the real world have certain mistaken notions, such as the patient who believes that he is a famous prizefighter or feels bugs crawling all over his body. The person grows attached to these ideas, and no amount of reasoning can change the conviction that they are real.

Being out of touch with reality, however, does not necessarily mean that psychotic individuals live in another world altogether. It just means that certain aspects of their lives are different. Psychotic people, unless they are in a period of extreme disorganization, know that they should get up in the morning, get dressed, eat three meals a day, and go to sleep at night. Bizarre actions, strange thoughts, or confused speech show a distortion of only a certain segment of reality. That is why psychotics may appear mentally ill at times and at other times seem perfectly normal.

Delusions and Hallucinations

In psychoses, thought distortions may result in *delusions,* which are strongly held beliefs that have no basis in objective fact. One patient in California, for instance, was convinced that San Francisco did not really exist. He insisted that it was created only for his visits and that each time he left it, it disappeared. Most psychotics who suffer delusions hold on to their beliefs stubbornly, despite the absurdity and lack of logic of these beliefs and in the face of all evidence to the contrary.

A common kind of delusion, called *delusion of reference,* is the belief of some persons that everything going on refers to them. When such people see a group of individuals talking, they assume that they are the topic of conversation and may become very excited and agitated.

A young hospitalized mental patient felt that he was under the control of an advanced electronic robot. He was convinced that the robot made him do things that he knew were wrong. This delusion, the *delusion of influence,* at times forced him to smash windows, break mirrors, and overturn furniture.

Psychotics who have *delusions of persecution* believe that enemies are trying to harm them, are plotting against them, are interfering in their lives, and are preventing them from achieving happiness and success. The popular image of a psychotic as a patient who believes that he is the president of the United States is an example of a *delusion of grandeur*. This type of delusion appears with some frequency among mental patients.

Other delusions include the patients' opinions that they have committed some horrible sin, which has brought great pain to others and which proves that they are worthless and evil. Then there are the *nihilistic delusions* in which the patients are convinced that nothing really exists in the world. Everything, including the individual, is just a shadow or a ghost.

Delusions are thoughts that have no basis in fact; *hallucinations* are experiences that have no basis in fact. Hallucinations are most often heard, but they may also be seen, felt, tasted, or smelled. The hallucinations, of course, come from within the psychotic's brain, but to the individual they seem to come from outside and to be very real.

Some psychotics report that they hear voices telling them what to do, accusing them of wicked sexual acts, criticizing them for what they have done, or threatening to harm them. The most frequent visual hallucinations involve seeing angels or devils. One patient told about seeing the sky and clouds, even though she was indoors and was not looking out the window. There are a few accounts of individuals in hospitals talking about and caring for pets that only they can see.

Some patients, though, suffer hallucinations that are encountered less often. Bugs, snakes, or other types of animals seem to be crawling on their skin, filling them with tremendous fear and loathing. A number believe that they are eating something with a disgusting taste. And some tell of detecting terrible smells, which they believe are poison gases.

Hallucinations are extremely frightening and upsetting experiences. Rational explanations and reassuring evidence that they do not exist do little to quiet the fears or calm the anxieties of patients. It usually requires intensive treatment to bring hallucinations under control.

Disordered Thoughts and Emotions

Thinking disorders or disturbances impair the psychotic's total vision of the world. A troubled adolescent boy, when interviewed by a psychiatrist, for example, was not able to stay with one thought for very long or to concentrate on one topic. He was easily distracted and jumped from one idea to another. If the psychiatrist crossed his legs or scratched his head, the young man became so disoriented that he forgot what he was saying.

Some patients have difficulty discriminating between different things going on in the environment. One mental patient tended to focus her attention on people across the room rather than on the speaker right next to her. Another was made very uncomfortable by the noise of traffic or of passing airplanes. As a result of poor discrimination and distractibility, patients with this disorder will often lose their concentration. They will leave off in the middle of a sentence or abandon a task before it is finished. This difficulty in thinking makes it hard for them to examine alternatives and make decisions. Many take an especially long time to react to questions or come up with answers.

Some sufferers with psychoses are unable to separate what is relevant from what is not. This sometimes leads people like Freddy, a psychotic patient, to sit alone and dwell on a single thought for hours. Because he does not seem to be able to connect thoughts into logical sequences, the result is disorganized and fragmented thinking. It is not unusual for Freddy to be talking about a serious matter and laughing about a remembered joke at the same time because of the jumble of thoughts in his mind. As Freddy puts it, "If I could only focus on one thing at a time I wouldn't look half so silly."

Thought disorders may make communication very difficult and lead to a worsening of the psychotic's condition. Even Freddy's mother and father find it hard to understand what he is saying, or even trying to say, so they tend to avoid contact with him. This makes Freddy feel even more isolated and out of touch with the real world.

Life for those suffering from psychotic disorders can be unbelievably confusing and frightening. Having lost a sense of reality, these people feel lonely and fearful. This impacts strongly on the way they behave. Psychiatrists use the term *emotional blunting* to describe how some patients withdraw into themselves, just staring out into space, unmoving, reluctant to dress or eat, and hardly talking at all. It is as though all of their thoughts and emotions have been deadened or blunted. Others, though, react in the opposite way, becoming hyperactive and moving about constantly, always busy, alert, and on the go. Or, in some instances, they alternate from one extreme to the other.

Schizophrenia

Of all the psychotic disorders, schizophrenia is the most widespread and is considered the most serious. About 2.1 million Americans are diagnosed as schizophrenics.

Psychiatrists say that most cases start to develop between adolescence and early adulthood; a small percentage begin between thirty and sixty-five years of age. Children sometimes show some of the same symptoms in a condition known as autism, but scientists are still studying the relationship of these behaviors in children to schizophrenia in adults.

The popular idea that schizophrenia is a split personality derives from the origin of the word—*schizo* means "split," *phrenia* means "mind." But from the time the term was first coined by the Swiss psychiatrist, Dr. Eugen Bleuler, in 1911, it has really meant a split between the individual's perception of reality and reality, not a Dr. Jekyll-Mr. Hyde switch in character.

Schizophrenia has long been regarded as a group of related mental disorders, not one specific illness. Dr. Edward J. Sachar, director of the New York State Psychiatric Institute, describes it as, "a vast wastebasket of all kinds of psychiatric diseases." It is, indeed, a complex disorder that affects all aspects of the sufferer's personality.

Different people express the symptoms of schizophrenia in various, and sometimes changeable, ways. Carol was a patient who was extremely withdrawn from personal contact, sometimes to the point of not talking at all. Sam was much more outgoing and responsive, but his thought processes, emotional reactions, and speech were all disorganized and confused. Jimmy heard threatening voices that were wholly imaginary and had frequent delusions that someone was trying to poison him. What they had in common was the profound disturbance, not of the same emotions and thoughts, but of their entire personalities.

Schizophrenia often starts when the person is quite young. Penny, for example, always seemed very slow and lazy to her parents and teachers. When asked her preference in a situation or to make a decision, she would usually say, "I don't care." As she approached adolescence she became even more aloof and more reticent. She never joined any clubs or took part in school affairs.

After Penny graduated from high school, she lost all interest in what she was doing and broke off all social contacts. She also began neglecting her appearance and personal hygiene. More and more she withdrew into her own fantasy world.

As time went on, she found it increasingly hard to concentrate or to carry through on any project. People sometimes heard her speaking when there was no one nearby. She also told of hearing voices that she found very frightening. Eventually Penny was hospitalized in the psychiatric division of the local hospital. The tests there confirmed that she was indeed suffering with schizophrenia.

Acute, or *undifferentiated, schizophrenia* is the most prevalent form of the disorder. It may strike quite suddenly and affect someone who had previously been thought completely normal. Harry is an example of a person who experienced such a breakdown. As a fourth-year medical student, he failed his exams, upsetting his fiancée so much that she canceled their wedding plans. Soon afterwards, his roommate found Harry on the floor of their apartment sobbing uncontrollably and speaking incoherently. Seeing Harry's dazed and confused condition, his friend called a doctor. The doctor and roommate decided to arrange for Harry's admission to a hospital. The psychiatrists there diagnosed Harry as suffering from acute schizophrenia.

For many days, all of Harry's thoughts were turned within. He seldom spoke and showed no interest in where he was or what he was doing. The least effort, even walking from one room to another, left him exhausted.

Then, with treatment, Harry started to come out of it. The doctors sent him home for longer and longer visits. Finally Harry was discharged. He stayed at home for a one-month rest before returning to school. The second time around he easily passed his exams and went on to become a successful doctor. The symptoms that sometimes recur and remain a lifelong threat never returned in his case.

Paranoid schizophrenia accounts for the second greatest

number of mental hospital admissions, next to cases of acute schizophrenia. This schizophrenic reaction often shows up as sets of changeable delusions and hallucinations, which can lead to bizarre, unpredictable, and sometimes dangerous, behavior. Paranoia, which most psychiatrists recognize as a separate condition, is like paranoid schizophrenia, but without a complete breakdown of personality.

Paranoid schizophrenia sufferers frequently have delusions of persecution. Friends, relatives, strangers, and foreigners may all be looked on with suspicion as potential enemies. Many patients who truly believe that others are out to harm them also come to believe that they must be pretty important to attract so much attention and hatred. As a result, some develop delusions of grandeur, becoming, in their own minds, powerful or world-famous figures. Frequently these delusions are accompanied by hallucinations. Some acutely troubled patients, such as a young man who heard voices urging him to attack and kill old men, may become physically violent.

One popular image we get from movies and television is of the *catatonic* type of schizophrenia. Withdrawal from their surroundings is so complete that patients suffering from this condition may be practically mute and may even remain fixed in one position for hours on end. It almost seems that by staying silent and immobile in a particular posture they are trying to maintain their fragile mental balance.

Catatonic schizophrenics sometimes undergo dramatic changes. Suddenly they become hyperactive, sometimes wild and frantic, perhaps shouting and moving uncontrollably at the same time. In such an acute state the patients are liable to harm either themselves or others.

What Causes Schizophrenia?

Scientists still do not know the cause of schizophrenia, nor do they agree on what conditions are most likely to produce the disorder. Opinions are divided among the "mind" supporters, who argue for emotional and psychological causes, and the "body" proponents, who blame heredity and biochemistry. Patients and their families are often bewildered and have trouble deciding which view has the most merit.

For most of this century, schizophrenia was believed to be caused by a poor upbringing and an unhappy home environment. The psychological impact of the stress, psychiatrists said, severely damaged the child's mental development and caused the symptoms of the illness to appear. This view required schizophrenics to work through their emotional conflicts. This "working through" proved to be very difficult or impossible for most patients. The results were often quite disappointing.

The use of mind drugs on schizophrenics in the 1950s, however, dramatically changed the behaviors of patients and helped to bring some of the symptoms of the illness under control. Many of the same patients then became able to benefit from psychiatric treatment. This discovery that brain chemistry may be related to the disorder led researchers in many directions as they sought medical or organic causes for schizophrenia.

One promising line of experimentation involves enzymes. Enzymes are protein molecules that control the millions of biochemical reactions that are constantly taking place in the body. For the last few years, several researchers in schizophrenia have been looking closely at an enzyme called monoamine oxidase, or MAO. MAO's function is related to the supply of a chemical that is responsible for the transmission of electrical messages between nerve cells in the brain and in the rest of the nervous system.

Since 1972, Dr. Richard Jed Wyatt of St. Elizabeth's Hospital in Washington, D.C., has been studying the amount of MAO in the blood. In some thirty studies involving schizophrenics, he has found a correlation between low MAO levels and chronic schizophrenia. As a matter of fact, the evidence seems to indicate that the lower the amount of MAO, the more serious the mental illness. One interesting research project showed that if one of a pair of identical twins is schizophrenic, the level of MAO is lower than normal in *both* twins. Unfortunately, low MAO activity is inconclusive in diagnosing patients, because it has also been found among subjects who are not schizophrenic.

Dr. Eugene Roberts of the City of Hope National Medical Center in Duarte, California, is examining evidence that a change in certain brain cells, the GABA neurons, as they are called, may be involved in schizophrenia. According to Dr. Roberts, some of the GABA neurons may be destroyed, or may not be functioning properly, for any number of reasons. This might lead to the release of too much dopamine, a chemical that plays a part in the transmission of messages throughout the nervous system, which in turn could produce disorganization and confusion. Dr. Roberts believes that the changes would probably produce schizophrenia only in a person who was already genetically predisposed to the condition.

Those who believe in heredity as a root cause of schizophrenia refer to evidence that shows a higher incidence of the illness among relatives of patients than among people in the general population. The incidence of schizophrenia among parents of schizophrenic children, for example, runs as high as 12 percent. In the general population the rate is only 1 percent. Further evidence is the fact that for identical twins, who have the exact same genetic makeup, the chances are about even that if one twin is schizophrenic, the other twin will be also. Yet for fraternal twins, who have different genetic factors, the likelihood is far lower.

While there may be a heredity factor, others argue that schizophrenia itself is probably not inherited. It may just be that the *predisposition* to schizophrenia is hereditary. The condition might then develop due to any number of reasons. Inheritance alone, they hold, is not likely to be the only factor responsible for schizophrenia.

Since most cases of schizophrenia are found among members of the lowest socioeconomic groups in our society, some suspect that the environment is a factor in the development of this disorder. Poverty, it is argued, is usually associated with poor nutrition and care before and after the birth of a child, which may increase the risk of schizophrenia. Children growing up in troubled or in broken homes, where there may be drug and alcohol abuse, problems with the law, and severe financial difficulties, may find it harder to achieve healthy emotional adjustments than youngsters raised in more well-ordered circumstances. However, some people suggest that schizophrenics are mostly found in low socioeconomic groups because the illness causes many to "drift down" from the higher groups.

Dr. Loren R. Mosher, chief of the National Institute of Mental Health Center for Studies of Schizophrenia, also points to the environment as a possible contributing cause of schizophrenia. He makes a comparison between schizophrenia and height or intelligence: "These are genetically influenced," he explains, "but there is no gene for height and none for intelligence. Multiple genes are involved, and environment has a tremendous influence. You may be predisposed to high intelligence, but if you are raised with poor nutrition and a poor environment, you may not grow up very smart."

Analysis of the geographical distribution of schizophrenia has led Dr. Seymour Kety of Harvard University to believe that a virus might play a role. Schizophrenia appears to occur much the same throughout the world. The only two exceptions are one area of northern Sweden and all of Ireland, where it is more common. Could it be that there is a virus, found in greater concentrations in these two places, which is somehow able to trigger schizophrenia?

The general conclusion right now seems to be, in the words of Dr. Nathan Kline, director of the Rockland Research Institute in Orangeburg, New York, "There is no 'schizococcus'—no single agent that causes schizophrenia."

Schizophrenia, considered to be the most complex mental disorder, may be the result of a combination of several causes. Severe emotional disturbances may occur in some because of an imbalance in the body's chemistry. In others it may be caused by a certain personality development or environmental pressure that combines with a particular hereditary predisposition towards the disease.

Schizophrenia, then, most experts agree, results from some faulty interaction between mind and body. As Dr. Silvano Arieti says in his book, *Interpretations of Schizophrenia,* "I believe there is a predisposition to schizophrenia, but the damage to the ego comes from psychological factors acting on a biologically vulnerable person."

Depressive Psychosis

An estimated 2 million Americans suffer from severe depression, according to recent estimates by the National Institute of Mental Health. During any one year, about 125,000 people are hospitalized with the symptoms of depression while another 200,000 receive treatment as outpatients. One survey of a random sample of adults from eighteen to seventy-five years of age showed that as many as 15 percent of the people questioned may have significant symptoms of depression. Severe depression is believed to be a contributing cause of more than 23,000 suicides every year.

The parents of Howard, a teenager with a depressive psychosis, described his symptoms this way: "Howard is almost always gloomy, hopeless, and withdrawn. He hardly moves at all, just sitting in one place, looking and sounding terribly tired all the time. Although we are quite well-to-do, Howard is convinced that we have no money and that it is his fault that we are poor."

Some depressive psychotics have recurring, or cyclical, depressive attacks that are not at all associated with any par-

46

ticular event. On these occasions they are so drained of strength and vitality that they are unable to accomplish even the simplest tasks. Others with this condition seem to suffer the depressive reactions when faced with a stressful situation. Even a minor crisis is sometimes enough to set off a serious, debilitating depressive episode.

Some psychiatrists say that the most common warning sign in depressive psychosis is an abrupt change in personality. A successful businessman suddenly loses his confidence, lets others make decisions for him, and blames himself whenever anything goes wrong in the company. All at once a devoted mother becomes terribly afraid that she is going to harm her children and spends most of her time in bed, saying, "I'm no good to anyone! I'm going to be dead soon."

Alice, a young homemaker, was severely depressed for a three-month period. She felt very sad, lonely, fearful, and guilt-ridden. She thought slowly, spoke hesitatingly and in a monotonous voice, and walked stoop-shouldered. Frequently she contemplated suicide.

Suddenly, one day, Alice's mood improved. She spoke more freely and appeared cheerful and optimistic. By the following day she was speaking almost without stop and was a whirlwind of physical activity, almost the complete opposite of her former self. Then she began saying strange things. She claimed that people were trying to kill her because she was smarter than they, and she argued loudly and violently with family members when they tried to calm her down. Over the next two days, her talkativeness and activity increased to the point where she was unable to control herself.

The family doctor was called, and Alice was hospitalized with the condition known as *manic-depressive psychosis*. This disorder, which usually strikes adults between twenty-five and sixty-five years of age, afflicts more females than males. In Alice's case the depressive phases, periods of deep sadness and lethargy, alternated with manic phases, periods of great elation and activity. Some patients show only manic behavior or only depressive behavior.

Sometimes the symptoms of depression can be hidden or confusing. A person may see a doctor frequently for vague complaints, such as chronic fatigue, that are found to be without any physical basis. An individual may use drugs or drink excessively. There does not seem to be any one symptom, or even any one combination of symptoms, that points with certainty to extreme depression.

Depressive disorders range from temporary reactions to loss or separation, to severe depressive illness. In almost any form, however, the condition is very disturbing, not only to the patient but to the family, too. In those patients who are suicidal, it may be a fatal illness as well.

Causes of Severe Depression

It is still not known for certain why some people become profoundly depressed for no obvious external reason or as recurrent reactions to stress. Most often the trigger seems to be a significant loss to the person, such as the death of someone close, a major problem at work, or a failing interpersonal relationship. But there is growing evidence that, just as with schizophrenia, genetic factors, biochemical imbalances, and the pressures of the environment may all play a part.

Studies show that depression is much more likely to occur in a person with a family history of depressive illness. Nearly 23 percent of depressed patients were found by National Institute of Mental Health investigators to have had mentally ill mothers, and more than 13 percent had depressed fathers.

Dr. William E. Bunney, Jr., chief of the Biological Psychiatry Branch of the National Institute of Mental Health, has found evidence for genetic and biological causes for depression in his studies of twins. Among fraternal twins, if one twin has depression, the other acquires it 13 percent of the time. Among identical twins, though, the figure is as high as 60 to 90 percent. The correlation is even high among identical twins who are separated at birth and raised in different environments.

Teams of scientists have been studying the chemical changes in the body that take place when a person enters a depressive state. They want to learn whether the altered chemistry is the cause of the depression or is caused by the depression.

Some tests found that a certain chemical excreted in the urine was markedly increased over long periods of time in patients who were severely depressed and suicidal. Could this so-called stress hormone be an indicator of depression and of future attempts at suicide? Some biochemical researchers are looking into these results or investigating other leads for diagnosing depressive psychoses.

A current research project induces depression in laboratory animals in order to learn more about the illness in humans. The experimenters are finding that young monkeys who are separated from their mothers at an early age and kept isolated take on many of the outward behavioral characteristics of human depression. Currently, the researchers are attempting to bring about behavioral changes in the animals by treating them with various drugs and chemicals.

Experiments with dogs have shown that when these animals learn that they can do nothing to avoid a mild but painful electric shock, they become passive, lie down, and accept their fate. Even when they are taught that a certain response can bring relief, the animals remain helpless. Since passivity and helplessness also characterize depressed humans, researchers hope to learn how individuals can be helped to realize that they can do something to help themselves.

Environmental pressures may increase the likelihood of depression. A stressful situation or event is closely linked to the actual onset of depression or mania. A husband asks for a divorce to marry another woman; a young family moves to California and leaves Grandmother alone in New York; a young athlete discovers that he has lung cancer; a son or daughter commits suicide. All these are examples of very stressful situations. One National Institute of Mental Health study found that each of forty depressed patients had suffered from a severe personal problem in the year preceding the appearance of his or her illness.

Overcooperative, overconscientious, and self-sacrificing persons seem particularly susceptible to depression according to Dr. Ari Kiev, a psychiatrist at the New York Hospital–Cornell Medical Center. Being afraid to express anger for fear of being rejected or making others angry, as well as holding unrealistic expectations for yourself and others, he believes, may also be contributing factors to depression.

Dr. Kiev has also said, "When families see the depression as the result of willfulness, an unwillingness to fight it off, then that tends to increase the patient's frustration. And it is in that kind of setting that one would see suicidal acts." It is estimated that as many as 75 percent of those who attempt suicide are seriously depressed.

Depressive psychosis, schizophrenia, and the other psychoses are the most serious of all mental disorders. They affect large numbers of people, bringing great suffering and anguish to them and to their families. Care and treatment can be very costly. Major research projects are going forward in nearly all countries of the world to try to point the way toward preventing, relieving, or even curing these terribly handicapping illnesses.

5
Other Mental Illnesses

There are about 1 million Americans currently suffering from disabling mental illnesses known to have a physical basis. Among such patients are the many elderly who suffer from senility, due to conditions that damage or destroy brain cells; persons with diseases such as syphilis, encephalitis, and multiple sclerosis; those with brain tumors or other injuries to brain tissue; and those with psychoses related to alcoholism or drug abuse.

Senility

There is virtually an "epidemic" of senility in America. About 5 percent of people over sixty-five show symptoms of memory loss, disorientation of time and place, and impaired thinking ability. An elderly sales manager for an insurance agency is so forgetful that she sometimes can't remember how to dress herself without help. A seventy-year-old farmer cannot find his way back to his house from his fields. A retired schoolteacher is not able to add up a column of numbers. People with such symptoms are often said to be suffering from *senile dementia.*

The prevailing view is that brain function does not necessarily decline with age. When older people develop such problems it is usually the result of one or more of the diseases that commonly strike the aged. One example is arteriosclerosis, or hardening of the arteries. This condition allows less blood to flow through the arteries and cuts the circulation of blood to the brain, resulting in injury to brain cells.

Strokes, or cerebral hemorrhages, which occur most frequently in older people, are caused by a break in the wall of one of the blood vessels in the brain. The result is damage to or the destruction of brain cells. The number of cases of senile behavior due to either arteriosclerosis or stroke, however, is limited to no more than about one out of five.

Recent research findings show that about half of the cases diagnosed as senile dementia are due to Alzheimer's disease. This disease, sometimes found in young people as well, has no known cause. Some believe that it is caused by a virus that damages or destroys brain cells; others suspect a deficiency in certain brain chemicals. Treatment is also unknown, and patients with this disorder usually become mentally helpless.

Depression neuroses often cause elderly people to behave like those with organic brain damage. Physicians frequently come up with a diagnosis of organic brain disease when a patient is actually depressed. Depression is one of the most widespread forms of mental illness among the aged, accounting for a great percentage of all mental illness in this group. Among others, Dr. Nancy Miller of the National Institute of Mental Health cites data suggesting that depression leads to changes in the ability to reason and impairment in short-term memory, though this is not always recognized by medical doctors.

Many elderly people show senile behaviors due to abuse or misuse of tranquilizers, barbiturates, and other kinds of mind-affecting drugs. One sixty-eight-year-old woman, in good physical and mental health, fractured her pelvis and was admitted to a nursing home in California to recover. Her doctor prescribed daily doses of certain medications that included tranquilizers and an antidepressant. She was also given sleeping pills. In less than a month this woman was reported as being "confused," "paranoid," and "mentally incompetent." Her daughter took her out of the nursing home and brought her into her own house. Away from all the medications, the woman soon recovered her good mental health. Studies have shown that errors are made in administering more than 25 percent of the medication given in nursing homes, and the chance of an elderly person being given the wrong drug or the wrong dose is said to be twice that of a thirty-year-old.

The symptoms of senility that are caused by arteriosclerosis and strokes or by Alzheimer's disease do not respond very well to treatment. But signs of depression can be relieved and often corrected, and drug abuse can be avoided. Improved ways of diagnosing senility in its earliest stages and better care for the elderly will undoubtedly help reduce the great numbers of older persons now in psychiatric health facilities.

Different Types of Brain Damage

Syphilis is a disease caused by a bacteria; encephalitis is usually caused by a virus. Both of these infectious diseases are curable, and if caught early enough and treated, they do not leave any permanent damage. Untreated, however, they can strike at the brain and leave the patient seriously and permanently mentally disabled.

In syphilis, where the resulting mental condition is called *paresis,* the disorder progresses from emotional blunting, excessive sentimentality, and a general carelessness in behavior to a total neglect of personal hygiene and, eventually, a complete personality breakdown. The symptoms of encephalitis, on the other hand, include fever, delirium, behavioral disorders, tremors, and finally a stupor. Because of the stupor, some forms of this disease are called sleeping sickness.

53

The onset of certain diseases, such as pneumonia, diphtheria, and uremia, causes the body to produce certain poisons, or toxins. Normally there is a barrier that prevents chemicals in the body from crossing over into the brain. In some cases, though, these toxins are able to cross the barrier. If they enter the brain, they can cause delirium, restlessness, feelings of unease, and a greatly heightened sensitivity to noise and light. Eventually, if no treatment is given, the patient becomes confused and disoriented. All of these diseases, though, respond to medication. As long as the illness is not too severe or long-lasting, the mental symptoms disappear once the disease is cured.

Tumors and head injuries can damage the brain and bring about either temporary or permanent changes in behavior or mental functioning.

One woman's family noticed that she was no longer able to keep score in the card games she had always enjoyed playing. They also became aware that she tired quickly and became confused much more easily. When they took her for a checkup, the physician found the cause of the difficulties, a brain tumor. During a lengthy operation, surgeons removed the tumor. Not long after, the woman resumed all her usual activities, including card playing.

A brain tumor is a growth of abnormal tissue within the brain. As the tumor grows in size and competes with the brain cells for space and blood supply, it often leads to a weakening of the memory, particularly short-term memory, and to depression, headaches, and sometimes seizures. Removing the tumor very often corrects the condition.

A severe blow to the head or a fall resulting in a concussion or fractured skull may cause a temporary period of unconsciousness. During the recovery period, as the person regains consciousness, there is often stupor and confusion, which may last a few minutes or up to several days. Almost everyone makes a complete recovery from such incidents. In rare instances, people may be left with headaches, anxiety, dizziness, or a weakened memory. Only the most severe cases leave the victims either with lessened intellectual ability or a noticeable personality disorder.

Alcoholism and Drug Abuse

Although almost 10 million people in the United States admit to having problems related to alcohol, only about 1 million receive treatment for alcoholism. Alcoholism is regarded as a disease by some and as a symptom of mental illness by others. Those who drink excessively are generally unable to control how much they drink and cannot function well physically, socially, or mentally. In addition to the physical and mental damage to the alcoholic, babies born to alcoholic mothers have a death rate eight times that of babies in general. Those that survive are apt to be mentally retarded.

Dan was a flute player in a leading symphony orchestra. For years he drank to feel relaxed, to curb his anxieties, to reduce his inhibitions, and at times to deaden various minor aches and pains. Gradually, however, the conductor and some of the other players noticed that Dan was showing the first symptoms of alcoholism—a lack of physical coordination and loss of sensation. Always an excellent musician, he was having difficulty playing his instrument and learning new music. At home, Dan was avoiding his family responsibilities, lying about how much he was drinking, and displaying chronic irritability. What is more, he had occasional visual hallucinations of animals that he thought were about to attack him.

Dan's alcoholism finally reached the point where he could no longer play the flute. He could not keep his sense of place and time, speak coherently, or even keep his hands and lips from trembling. In desperation he agreed to enter a treatment program. His psychiatrist prescribed minor tranquilizers to control his worst symptoms. Through individual psychotherapy and counseling, he was helped to get at the root causes of his illness. Eventually Dan joined Alcoholics Anonymous, a self-help group made up of recovered alcoholics, and regained his position as an orchestra musician.

Heavy users of narcotics (heroin), psychedelics (marijuana, PCP, LSD), and stimulants (cocaine, amphetamines) often become psychologically dependent on the drug. In time they may develop an addiction, which is a strong physical need for the substance. The symptoms of drug abuse vary widely according to the substance, the amount, and the person's history. Most drugs, though, bring about changes in mood and personality and sometimes lead to hallucinations. When mixed with alcohol, the effects may be even worse and endanger life itself.

The favored method of treatment for drug abuse seems to be to wait out the acute phase and then either to diminish the amount of the drug gradually or to substitute a less harmful substance for the drug. Treatments where methadone has been used to replace heroin have been highly publicized. During most drug treatment programs, help is also given to build up the drug user's physical health and counseling is provided to strengthen the person psychologically.

The results, though, are not too encouraging. The U.S. Public Health Service and other treatment centers report that up to 85 percent of drug addicts become addicted again after completing treatment. Some new techniques, however, that are just becoming available are promising much better results than this figure indicates.

6

Treating Mental Illness

Psychotherapists have a bewildering number of ways to treat mental disorders. The treatment that is chosen is usually the one that the therapist believes will be most helpful to the patient. Generally, the treatment takes one of two main directions. The *psychotherapies* use talk between patient and therapist as the main means of uncovering the hidden sources of illness. The *organic therapies* depend mostly on drugs, special diet, electroshock, or psychosurgery to control or relieve the symptoms of the mental disturbance. In some cases, the particular course of treatment includes a combination of both principal types of therapy.

Talking It Out

Psychoanalysis is the granddaddy of all verbal, or talking, therapies. Originated by Sigmund Freud around 1900, the approach encourages and guides patients to talk freely and then to analyze what they said. The goal is to bring out the hidden feelings and unresolved conflicts of childhood that psychoanalysts believe are the sources of emotional difficulties. Once patients understand and accept the causes of their problems, they are on their way to better mental health.

Free association is a major tool of the psychoanalysts.

Patients are encouraged to let their minds wander and to say whatever occurs to them as a way of revealing their unconscious thoughts. In dream analysis, patients recount their dreams, and try, with the aid of the psychiatrist, to gain insights into their feelings and thoughts.

Sometimes during psychoanalysis, the patient develops resistance to the process. He or she may become angry with the analyst, forget appointments, or leave out important details in relating dreams, for example. The successful completion of treatment depends on the patient's finding ways to overcome this resistance.

After a time, some people in analysis begin unconsciously to transfer strong emotions that they once felt for parents or other important figures to the analyst. A woman may fear and hate the analyst the way she feared and hated her father when she was a young girl. A man may want to kill his analyst just as he once wanted to kill his older brother. Patients reach the end of treatment when they are able to handle their conflicts without great discomfort and without resorting to unhealthy methods of coping.

Psychoanalysis usually requires one or more fifty-minute sessions a week. It can take many years and cost thousands of dollars. Psychiatrists find analysis much more useful in treating neuroses than psychoses. Also, they find that the success rate is higher with YAVIS—*Y*oung, *A*ttractive, *V*erbal, *I*ntelligent, *S*uccessful individuals. Since so few people are YAVIS, it is not surprising that a number of other psychotherapies have grown out of Freud's basic psychoanalytic method.

One approach tries to speed up psychoanalysis by having the analyst play a much more active role in the process. Take the instance of a young singer who was preparing for her debut at the Metropolitan Opera and suddenly became so apprehensive that she was unable to practice or rehearse. Rather than slowly try to uncover the roots of her problem, the psychotherapist used a form of rapid treatment that is sometimes called STAPP (Short-Term Anxiety-Provoking Psychotherapy). He asked her probing questions that made her feel anxious and uncomfortable: "Imagine that you make a mistake on opening night. What would happen?" and, "Are you so frightened because you really want to fail?" The therapist then helped the singer confront the causes of her anxiety and helped her work through to an understanding and a solution. After only eight sessions, the vocalist felt well enough to resume working and to face her upcoming performance.

Sometimes people have shocking or painful experiences which they repress, or erase, from their conscious thought. The repressed memories may influence the person's behavior and cause certain forms of mental illness. Psychotherapists occasionally use hypnosis to help individuals recall incidents or situations that they had completely forgotten, to bring about a change in their behavior.

Group therapy is psychotherapy that takes place when a single therapist works with a number of patients at the same time. Many actually find it easier to talk their problems out in a group than alone with a therapist. They seem to be helped by knowing that others have similar problems. Interaction between the people in the group as well as between patient and therapist makes it closer to a real-life situation.

Quite often transference is made to members of the group. The individual member may actually express and work out the hostilities, fears, tensions, and anxieties that led to the symptoms of mental illness.

Psychodrama is one form of group therapy where people have a chance to act out their feelings as a means of gaining insights into their behavior. One woman at a group therapy session in a Chicago mental health clinic told the others how her mother had severely beaten her when she was twelve years old. Afterwards she had recurring thoughts of killing her mother, followed by strong feelings of guilt.

59

With another group member playing the part of the mother, the woman reenacted the incident. The leader then suggested a reversal of roles so that the troubled woman played her mother. Different members of the group made comments and told of similar childhood experiences. Being able to relive the experience, talk about it, and hear the reactions of others helped the woman discover feelings that she was not aware of before treatment.

To enjoy relationships with others, you must be genuinely able to share experiences. Many people find this very hard to do. *Sensitivity training groups,* sometimes called T groups, help individuals to overcome distrust of others and get in better touch with their own feelings. *Encounter groups,* too, aim to bring down the defenses established in childhood that prevent people from enjoying meaningful adult relationships with others.

Donna and Frank attend an encounter group together. They say that the free expression of feelings and the honest reactions of others help them heighten their awareness of themselves as they really are. "It can be both pleasurable and painful," Donna says. "You know you've made it when a light goes on in your head and you suddenly realize what the trouble has been."

Primal therapy is a group approach that assumes that neurotics were never fully able to express their anger at being left alone, rejected, or unloved as infants. The therapist aims to help the adults relive the damaging situations by making them feel miserable and isolated. When the distress becomes too great, the patient lets out all his or her pent-up anger in a "primal scream." The object is to free the emotions so that the person feels better.

According to *transactional therapy,* people have trouble getting along because in the social games they play they are acting out different parts of their personalities. These three parts, or ego states, are the child, mainly interested in pleasure; the parent, deciding what is good and bad; and the adult, the sensible, rational being. For example, one person's child part can't communicate with another's adult part. By understanding how all three parts of the personality work in social situations, people can be helped to achieve better interpersonal relations.

Most group therapies involve small groups of people and stretch out over long periods of time. The Erhard Seminars Training, or est, is for groups of over 200 people and lasts for only sixty hours over two weekends and three evenings. Participants are made physically uncomfortable by being required to forego eating and going to the toilet, for example. This deprivation presumably makes everyone better able to accept the message of est, with which they are repeatedly bombarded: "If you are willing to acknowledge that you are the cause of your own experience, then you can run your own lives instead of being run by them."

Closely related to group therapy is *family therapy*. An entire family meets with a therapist to discuss and seek solutions to common difficulties. Typically, a psychiatric social worker meets with the families of individuals who are undergoing psychotherapy. A father may need to spend more time alone with his troubled son. A wife may be harping too much on things her husband does without realizing that he is upset over a fear of losing his job. The family, simply by talking about their problems, may arrive at ways of improving the home situation for everyone and especially for the disturbed person.

Many patients require therapy more often than a few hours at a time or a few times a week. Therefore, many hospitals and other facilities offer round-the-clock *milieu therapy*. Milieu therapy attempts to change the environment, or milieu, in which a patient lives by placing that individual in a sequence of different surroundings. Highly trained people help the patient to utilize the well-equipped facilities. Activities range from arts and crafts to sports and recreation. Patients may be encouraged to become more responsible for their behavior, for helping others, and even for playing a role in the hospital's operation.

The person's reactions to each milieu are noted and changes are made in the environment to try to bring about the desired reactions. Many patients who do not respond well to any particular "talking treatment" improve with this approach. Too often, though, the term "milieu therapy" is used simply as a fancy term for what amounts to custodial care.

Changing Behavior
from the Outside In

What if anxiety, tension, fear of high places, and other kinds of neurotic behavior are treated as the problems, not the symptoms, of mental illness? What if they are regarded as learned responses to difficult situations? Then couldn't a therapist help the patients to unlearn this poor behavior, get rid of the bad habits and substitute good, healthy responses and ways of behaving—without worrying about any deep-rooted cause lurking in the patient's unconscious? That is, indeed, the basic position of many behavioral therapists.

One six-year-old child refused to go to school because he complained that he had a severe pain in his side. His very concerned mother took him to a doctor. A careful medical examination failed to show up any physical cause for the complaint. Since medication was not necessary, and even short-term psychoanalysis seemed excessive, behavior therapy was suggested.

Using a technique of *behavior modification,* the therapist advised the mother not to comfort or console the child when he complained and to show only a minimal interest in and concern for the physical symptoms. Instead, the therapist suggested that the mother pay attention to and spend time with him when he was not complaining.

At first, the boy insisted on the pain louder and more often. After several days, the number of complaints fell off. Soon they disappeared completely, and the boy began attending school regularly.

Behavioral techniques can help people who suffer phobic neuroses. Take the case of a college student who had claustrophobia. The girl was fearful of elevators, of small rooms, even of being surrounded by a crowd. She would climb many flights of stairs rather than use an elevator. The difficulty was traced back to a time when she had been caught up in a large group of students greeting a visiting politician. She reported such an overwhelming fear of suffocating that she panicked. Screaming loudly, she pushed her way out of the building and fled.

The behavior therapist used a common technique called *desensitization* to teach the young woman how to replace her tension about being caught in closed spaces with feelings of relaxation.

First the therapist taught the girl a method of relaxing the muscles of her body. Then he asked the student to list a number of situations in order, starting from the most anxiety-provoking to the most relaxing. At the top of the list was the fear of being locked up in a small room. Last was spending an afternoon at the beach.

Treatment began with the therapist's description of a very pleasant beach scene. As expected, the girl felt no tension at all. Then he painted a word picture of an area of her college campus that made her feel slightly uncomfortable. As he spoke, he urged her to use her relaxation techniques to gain control over even the tiny bit of anxiety that she was feeling.

At each session he took her step-by-step to more threatening places. All the while he helped her to maintain her relaxed state. After two months, she could imagine herself in a tiny, crowded elevator—and feel no tension or anxiety. Eventually she was able to enter those places that had caused her so much anguish and remain in control of her phobic fears.

Biofeedback, sometimes used with desensitization, employs electronic instruments to measure body functions, such as pulse or muscle tension, and makes this information available to the individual. Patients who suffer anxiety, for instance, watch a dial that shows their pulse rate increase or hear a tone that rises as their muscles tighten up. Once they can detect their own anxiety they are taught various ways to control these largely unconscious reactions.

Not long ago a study reported some success in controlling severe migraine headaches using biofeedback techniques. Subjects in the experiment learned to control their blood circulation, thereby relieving some of the migraine pain. In another recent experiment a girl was trained to use biofeedback to control her brain waves. Every time she generated alpha waves—a pattern of electricity in the brain—a loudspeaker emitted a soft tone. In time she found she could generate the alpha waves at will, giving her the ability to induce in herself a Yogalike state of inner peace and serenity.

The prospect of people learning to control their involuntary body processes is no longer a remote possibility. Some find the questions that it raises very troubling. What will be the consequences of such control? Will behavior therapy confine further advances to treating the patterns of behavior associated with mental illness, or will it create a society where human drives are brought under the control of researchers and therapists?

Psychotherapies of these various kinds are doubtless of value. But just how helpful they are in every case is impossible to predict or to determine. Many people, especially those most concerned with the treatment of severe mental illnesses, believe that none of the psychotherapies alone are effective as basic treatments. Most patients and families of seriously affected mental patients are advised, therefore, to look into various other forms of therapy as well.

Drug Therapy

Just three decades ago, even the most humane hospitals had to use straitjackets and padded cells to protect highly disturbed patients from injuring themselves or others. Depressive psychotics who seemed incapable of speaking, eating, or even standing up and walking were left untreated. And many neurotics who were unhappy or distressed had to struggle to keep their jobs or attend school.

The introduction of mind- and behavior-altering drugs revolutionized treatment of psychoses and neuroses. With these drugs most agitated patients can be calmed, most depressed patients can receive relief, and many neurotics can be helped to function better.

Such psychoactive drugs are usually divided into three groups. The antipsychotic drugs, or *major tranquilizers,* are the ones used to treat severe psychotic disorders. Among the most popular of these are chlorpromazine (Thorazine), haloperidol (Haldol), and thioridazine (Mellaril). These powerful drugs can quiet the disordered thoughts and hallucinations of schizophrenics, control violent behavior, and bring a patient out of a state of complete withdrawal.

Frank, a forty-seven-year-old factory worker, was in a hospital with acute schizophrenia. He frequently had hallucinations that set him off into violent rages. A daily regime of a major tranquilizer, however, eliminated most of his troubling behaviors. By combining the drug therapy with group therapy, the doctors were able to discharge Frank from the hospital and return him to his family and job.

The drugs used to treat severe depression are called either *antidepressants* or *energizers.* Some of the best known are doxepin (Sinquan), imipramine (Tofranil), and amitriptyline (Elavil).

Sally spent all of her time slumped in a chair in the day room of a Texas mental hospital. She never spoke, never moved, and seemed not to notice what was going on around her. If she was not led to the dining room, she would never have eaten. On a daily dose of antidepressants, however, Sally became friends with the other patients and began to take an interest in hospital activities.

Lithium salts, such as lithium carbonate, are neither major tranquilizers nor antidepressants. Yet they have been found to be very effective in treating the wild mood swings of manic-depressive psychosis. The drug calms the patient during a manic episode and energizes the same individual while in a depressed state. It also helps to prevent violent swings from one extreme to the other.

The *minor tranquilizers* are the drugs that are used to reduce anxiety and tension in people with neurotic symptoms. Diasepam (Valium), chlordiazepoxide (Librium), and meprobromate (Miltown) are the most frequently prescribed minor tranquilizers. About one out of every ten adult Americans takes one of the minor tranquilizers every year.

Marion is the mother of a five-year-old boy and three-year-old girl twins. They are all normal, healthy, active children, and Marion finds it very hard to keep up with them. She is often irritable and moody and gets angry at the children, often for no reason at all. When Marion discussed the problem with her doctor, he prescribed a minor tranquilizer to help her get through the rough days. He assured her that as the children grew older, it would be easier for her and she would probably not need the pills any more.

Drugs, and in particular the antipsychotic drugs, are now the main treatment for severe mental illness for the simple reason that they help patients lead more normal lives faster than any other method. But they are coming under increasing attack by mental patients, psychiatrists, and others, who say that the drugs are used mostly to control and stupefy the people in mental hospitals. On September 14, 1979, to take one example, inmates of New Jersey's five state mental hospitals sued the state for the right to refuse treatment with psychoactive drugs. The judge ruled that the patients do not have to accept such treatment.

There is also mounting evidence of serious physical and mental side effects of drug therapy. Antipsychotic drugs, when used over a long period of time, can cause permanent brain damage, resulting in a disfiguring and disabling condition known as tardive dyskinesia. Presently, though there are some ways to help people who have tardive dyskinesia, there is no cure, or prospect of cure, for this condition.

Eddy, a middle-aged mental patient on drug therapy since he was twenty, shows the symptoms of tardive dyskinesia. His speech is slurred, and there is an involuntary twitching of his lips, tongue, and facial muscles. Other serious side effects are a rigidity and stiffness in his body, a general slowness of movement, and lowered blood pressure.

As many as half the patients receiving antipsychotic drugs may be affected by tardive dyskinesia, according to one authority writing in the *Journal of the American Medical Association*. Women, the elderly, and brain-damaged patients show the highest incidence of the disorder.

Doctors are not always able to predict how a patient will respond to any given drug. In some cases, giving the wrong drug or an incorrect dosage can result in a condition worse than that which the drug was meant to cure. Administering an antidepressant to a schizophrenic has been likened to pouring gasoline on a fire.

Also, there is a possibility of addiction in patients who receive drug therapy. A recently divorced woman was given a prescription for a drug to treat her insomnia. She slept better but began having horrible dreams. Her doctor gave her a second drug to stop her nightmares. Gradually, as her body grew accustomed to the drugs, she needed to take two pills for a good night's sleep. As she became more and more dependent on the pills, she had to go from doctor to doctor to get new prescriptions. After two years, she was taking eight pills a night and showing signs of mental confusion and distorted thinking.

In one study, a group of patients were asked to contrast their experiences off and on drug therapy. In general, those on drugs felt more comfortable and less frightened; but they also cared less about their circumstances and felt more helpless about their future. Off drugs, most had more anxiety, sleeplessness, and feelings of panic, but there was a sense of being in control of their fate and more interest and drive to improve.

Some critics of drug therapy charge that drugs are often used merely because they are cheap and convenient, not because they help patients. When funds and staff in a psychiatric institution are limited, drugs are frequently substituted for rehabilitation and recreational activities.

Drugs, therefore, do not seem to be the whole answer to treatment either. They certainly have relieved some of the problems and enabled the return of patients to the outside world, but they have not cured anyone. A significant percentage of patients respond, but there are still many who do not or who have relapses. Is it wise to allow people to live permanently on maintenance doses of drugs, with the risk of harmful side effects? This is a very unsettling question. As more is learned about these potent chemicals and their risks, psychiatrists are becoming more cautious in prescribing them, and patients in taking them.

Orthomolecular Psychiatry

Ortho means "right," and *molecular* means "on the level of molecules." *Orthomolecular psychiatry,* which is based on the medical or organic model of mental illness, holds that mental disorders spring from improper balances of chemicals within the brain. The treatment approach is intended to provide the best possible balance of substances normally found in the body.

Marty had been smoking marijuana and taking hard drugs, such as heroin, since he was thirteen years old. He had been hospitalized several times and placed on methadone programs but went right back on heroin as soon as he was discharged. At age twenty-three he was placed under the care of an orthomolecular psychiatrist and given massive doses of vitamins, minerals, and protein supplements.

After three days, Marty reported a greatly diminished desire for the drug and said he was eating and sleeping better. The dosage was reduced, and after three months he was completely free of his dependence on heroin. He took a vocational training course and soon became employed for the first time in his life.

The scientific basis for Marty's treatment by orthomolecular means was established in the 1950s, when a number of cases of acute schizophrenia were treated by a combination of electroshock therapy and huge doses of vitamin B_3. The reported results were much better than those obtained with electroshock alone, with greater improvement in behavior for longer periods of time and with less loss of memory.

One explanation for these results is that most schizophrenics have a history of poor diet, and many are found to be suffering from hypoglycemia, or low blood sugar. This disorder of the metabolic system leads to such symptoms as depression, anxiety, phobias, and irritability. Since hypoglycemia is treated through diet, and there is some evidence that it is connected in some way with schizophrenia, it follows that diet might be a valid approach to the treatment of schizophrenia and perhaps other mental disorders.

Orthomolecular research on drug addiction has shown that many drug addicts have a defective gene for the production of a particular enzyme. The lack of this enzyme results in a shortage of vitamin C and a chemical the body needs for handling stress situations. Since drugs such as heroin relieve the anxiety of stress, these people are attracted to drugs and quickly become addicts. Further, heavy drug use reduces the appetite so much that many addicts are actually suffering from malnutrition or starvation which, by itself, may cause confusion and other symptoms of mental disorder. Therefore, according to the orthomolecularists, the treatment of drug addiction should include heavy doses of the various vitamins and minerals an addict's body is not able to produce, along with protein supplements to reverse the malnutrition.

There are, however, many psychiatrists who do not accept the theories of the orthomolecular psychiatrists and dispute their research findings. Both sides in this argument are continuing their studies to accumulate evidence that, they hope, will shed more light on this matter.

Electroshock and Psychosurgery

Before the introduction of drug therapy, the most common treatment for severe psychotic illness was electroshock therapy, known today as *electroconvulsive therapy (ECT)*. About 100,000 Americans a year receive ECT treatment. In ECT the patient is anesthetized, and then an electrical current is painlessly applied to the skull, causing a convulsive seizure. It is used today mostly on patients with extreme depressive illness or those in danger of committing suicide and on acute schizophrenics suffering disturbing delusions or hallucinations. The patient usually does not remember the treatment or the events that came just before. Often, though, severely disturbed patients who receive ECT show remission of symptoms in six to eight treatments, although nobody understands exactly why.

Those who favor ECT point out that modern ECT is generally safe and is a far cry from the horrors shown in some popular movies set in mental hospitals. For some seriously ill patients, who do not respond to drugs or who have disorders caused by the lengthy use of drugs, it is the only treatment that works. Half of the ECT patients questioned in one survey said that they were less afraid of the treatment than of going to the dentist.

Critics of ECT say that it can result in permanent brain damage, including a loss of long-term memory. A 1978 report by the American Psychiatric Association states that one-third of all psychiatrists have some reservations about the use of ECT and prefer, whenever possible, to use some other form of therapy. The author Ernest Hemingway said that ECT treatments ruined his career as a writer because they wiped out the memory of all past experiences. Marilyn Rice, who had been an economist, claims that ECT treatments ruined her expert knowledge in the field and forced her to retire from her job. One instance of serious opposition to ECT was seen at a recent psychiatric conference in Britain, where pickets carried signs reading, CONTROL PSYCHIATRY WHILE YOU STILL HAVE A MIND TO.

The treatment method that always arouses the greatest controversy is brain surgery, or *psychosurgery*. The purpose is to cut nerve pathways in the brain in order to alter behavior. About 200 to 400 such operations are performed in the United States every year. Psychosurgery is done only on patients with severe depression or other completely disabling conditions, on whom all other treatment methods have been used and failed, and where there is no likelihood of improvement in time.

One recent account of psychosurgery tells of a twenty-nine-year-old college graduate who suffered chronic depression and anxiety for five years. He sobbed convulsively for no known reason, had fits of panic, and exhibited a deep phobic fear of choking. Neither repeated hospitalizations, six different forms of psychotherapy, nor various drug therapies

71

helped him to any marked extent. In 1977 he was recommended for psychosurgery.

The surgeon inserted thin wire electrodes through two tiny holes in his skull. Pulses of electricity were sent to four separate targets in his brain, destroying tiny bits of tissue. Today the former patient is married and is working as a psychiatric nurse in a state hospital.

Dr. T. Corwin Fleming of Harvard Medical School estimates that more than 50 percent of all patients treated by psychosurgery show marked improvement and only a few are made worse. On this basis, believers in the procedure assert that to withhold treatment is to condemn a patient to a life of misery or suicide, and to block research is to deprive others of hope.

On the other hand, opponents argue that psychosurgery is unsafe and ineffective. The operation may lead to irreversible personality changes, they say, and there are other, less hazardous methods of treating the very sick. They claim that psychosurgery is a form of mind and thought control that has no place in a free society. While they agree that research in the field should be pursued, they insist that no humans should be made victims of the operation.

7

Aftercare and Rehabilitation

Throughout history, people with mental disorders have been excluded from society. For over a hundred years in America, most of the mentally ill have been confined in large state hospitals.

Very gradually, in the last few decades, the idea emerged that most of those found to be mentally ill do not need to be restrained or locked up in hospitals. These people posed no real threat either to society or to themselves. Often, the large institutions to which they were confined were human warehouses, where the patients received little or no treatment. Patients did not improve while there; many even became more disturbed as a result of their long confinements. In some cases, the long years of hospitalization resulted in mental retardation. Patients lost the ability to order and control their own lives and actions and were reduced to lifelong dependency.

The belief grew that large mental institutions were doing as much harm as good. Many psychiatrists held that patients would do better in smaller, less-structured community settings near their homes, families, and friends. Outside the oppressive institutional environments they would still be able to receive the help and treatment they needed to become independent. The way was paved for a new chapter in the aftercare of the mentally ill.

Deinstitutionalization

The introduction of psychoactive drugs in the 1950s offered the first real alternative to confinement in mental hospitals. The new drugs helped the patients to feel less anxiety, to suffer less from violent changes of mood, and to get over acute episodes of severe mental illness. Such treatment allowed patients to receive care outside of the hospital in settings close to where they lived before being hospitalized.

The concept to move patients out of the large, remote state hospitals received its biggest boost in 1963 when President John F. Kennedy signed the Community Mental Health Centers Act into law. The law mandated that all patients who did not need to be confined should be released from institutions, or deinstitutionalized. A national network of community health centers was to be set up with federal money. In time, it was hoped, funding would be taken over by local government.

The centers were to provide patients with a treatment program, including counseling near their homes and medication. This would allow them to function on their own in the least restrictive environment. It was thought that most patients would return to their families and communities. They would live at home or in special residences and receive treatment in the centers, putting an end to segregation in institutions.

Since deinstitutionalization was begun, the total population in all mental hospitals has decreased 65 percent in the twenty-two-year period between 1955 and 1977 (the last year figures are available). (See Table 3.)

Massachusetts, for example, closed three of its eleven state mental hospitals. Newly admitted patients stayed an average of three weeks, as compared to much longer periods in previous years. Whereas thirty years ago three out of four mental patients were being treated in hospitals, today only one out of four is confined to an institution.

74

Table 3.   **Trends in Patient Care**

Percent Distribution of Patients in Mental Health Facilities by Type of Program

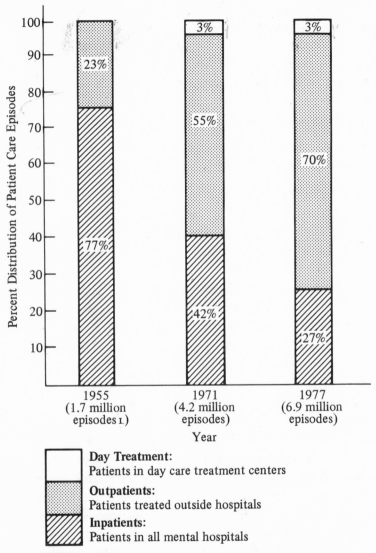

Day Treatment:
Patients in day care treatment centers

Outpatients:
Patients treated outside hospitals

Inpatients:
Patients in all mental hospitals

I. The number of patients at the beginning of the year *plus* the total additions during the year, which include new admissions, readmissions, and returns from leave.

Source: Division of Biometry and Epidemiology, NIMH, 1980.

With governments short of money, however, funds for sufficient community mental health centers and other aftercare facilities just did not materialize. Nearly half of the centers that were supposed to be established were never actually set up. Most people agree that after more than twenty years of de-institutionalization there are too few programs to meet the needs of mental patients. In addition, released patients who attempt to settle in residential neighborhoods continue to encounter community fear and resistance to the extent that neighbors sometimes band together to keep them out.

Adult Homes

While many former mental patients have managed well when returned to the community and have benefited from deinstitutionalization, far more have not. Forty-two-year-old Carl is an example of one who has suffered as a result of the new policy.

Carl lived in psychiatric hospitals for more than twenty years of his life. Diagnosed as schizophrenic by the doctors, Carl underwent ECT, drug therapy, and some counseling in the hospital. Under the present laws, which state that unless patients are under intense short-term treatment or are dangerous to themselves or others they must be released from mental hospitals, Carl was discharged and placed in a so-called adult home.

The "home" was formerly a small, run-down hotel that was located in a depressed part of Atlanta, Georgia, and was operated for profit by the owners. Carl was told to report once a week to a local hospital's aftercare clinic for an interview with a therapist and to receive a week's supply of the drug he takes to control his symptoms.

Carl found it very hard to manage. Without supervision, he often failed to take his medicine. His room was dirty and depressing, he suffered from malnutrition, and whenever he fell sick, he failed to get medical attention. Without protection, Carl was beaten and robbed several times.

After three visits to the clinic, Carl stopped coming. The overworked staff at the clinic had little time to track him down and find out why he was missing his appointments. Two months after his release, a police officer found Carl sleeping in a doorway. His clothes were torn and stained, he was missing several teeth, and he was in a dazed and confused condition.

Carl was returned to the hospital, where they discovered that he had taken a combination of another discharged patient's tranquilizers and cheap wine. A few weeks later he was discharged again. After a couple of weeks at the adult home, he again disappeared. Presently his whereabouts are unknown.

One report says that adult homes, called board and care homes in California, are little different from the wards in state hospitals, except that they are less closely supervised. Another study found no improvement in the ability of ex-patients to make decisions, handle money, or socialize with others, after living for a period of time in an adult home. An investigation revealed that four such homes were operated by one woman who earned $250,000 a year from government assistance checks. The former mental patients lived in foul conditions without adequate food, clothing, or personal care.

The cutbacks on long-term hospital confinement on the one hand, and the lack of community resources on the other, are catching some ex-patients like Carl in the middle. In most mental hospitals today, the focus is on short-term treatment and release. Kings County Hospital in Brooklyn, New York, as an example, has only ninety beds for psychiatric patients. Yet the hospital admits 6,000 acutely psychotic patients every year. The average stay, therefore, is about ten days, less than half the national average. Of these discharged patients, half are readmitted, either at the request of their families or by order of the courts.

"We're like a revolving door," says Martin S. Kessel-man, Kings County Hospital's director of psychiatric services. "There's no time to reach a patient before he's snatched away." Like many others all over the country, these men and women who are discharged from hospitals, left without help or care on the outside, and then returned to the hospitals, have been dubbed "revolving door patients."

Halfway Houses

While in college, a young woman named Lori had a serious mental breakdown and was admitted to a state mental hospital. Her condition improved enough for her to work as a clerk in the hospital while still a patient. In line with the trend toward community care, Lori was eventually discharged. A psychiatric social worker found her a place to live in a neighborhood halfway house for former mental patients.

A typical halfway house has room for between ten and twenty ex-patients. The house is not nearly as large as a hospital nor as small as a family apartment. Day-to-day responsibilities for running the house belong to a live-in couple who may be called houseparents or managers.

The husband and wife who managed Lori's halfway house treated the twenty residents like members of a large extended family. The members met often to talk about running the house and to solve any psychological or adjustment problems that cropped up. All were expected to pitch in with the shopping, cleaning, and cooking chores and were responsible for caring for themselves and for others.

The social worker who continued to see Lori arranged for her to enroll in a course to learn computer operation. After four months, the supervisors at the residence decided that the young woman was ready to move into her own apartment. When Lori had completed the computer course, she was helped to find a job as a computer operator. Now she lives in her own apartment and seems free of the symptoms that sent her to the hospital in the first place. She is even beginning to think of returning to college.

Residences such as the halfway houses have helped many discharged patients, such as Lori, make the transition from institutions to independence. Most halfway houses encourage contact with neighbors and other members of the community. House members shop in stores, attend schools, go to movies, use the library, and engage the services of physicians, dentists, plumbers, and electricians—all within the local area.

One of the main concerns in the halfway house is helping the discharged patients to find jobs. Fountain House in New York City, one of the oldest and most successful of the halfway houses, takes full responsibility for its members' jobs. The house director locates suitable positions for house members, assigns workers, trains them, supervises the trainees, and helps to solve any problems that arise.

The Fountain House program also tries to place members in living accommodations outside the house as soon as possible. Most only live in the house a month or two before they move out on their own. Living outside the house, though, does not mean severing all ties. Most members return to the house during the day or evening, as well as on weekends, for therapy, counseling, or basic education courses.

Various other centers for released mental patients offer their own special programs. Horizon House in Philadelphia, for instance, emphasizes vocational rehabilitation and socialization. Founded in 1953, the facility trains clients in everyday living skills, including help with personal hygiene, instructions on how to dress and shop, and the use of public transportation. The focus of Thresholds in Chicago is to improve social skills. The staff provide group activities within the facility and outside, including planned socialization experiences with friends, family, and members of the opposite sex.

Dr. Richard Budson of the Harvard Medical School says

that the successful operation of a halfway house depends on the enforcement of two basic rules. The first forbids the taking of any illicit drugs. Such activity could seriously impede the members' return to good mental health and might force the house to close. The other requires everyone to attend the house meetings. The reactions of the entire group to general, as well as personal, matters helps everyone strengthen his or her own life skills.

Regrettably, there are very few halfway houses. About 800 have been opened across the entire country. Perhaps that is why so many individuals are turning to self-help organizations for assistance.

Self-Help

After a December 1975 decision was reached which stated that over 1,300 patients of St. Elizabeth's Hospital in Washington, D.C., could and should be living in the community, a small staff and several ex-patients opened The Green Door, a clubhouse for members. Of major importance to ex-patients coming from a hospital environment was learning how to carry on conversations with others. Members also prepared for employment by doing jobs related to running the club, including office work.

Often the people that make self-help groups tick are not mental health professionals but former patients and concerned individuals in the community. Members counsel one another, hold meetings to exchange views on ways to work through various problems, and help one another set realistic goals. By stressing the shared nature of their problems and the fact that they are not alone, members help one another work their way out of dependency and helplessness.

Three of the most active self-help groups are Recovery, made up of released mental patients and people diagnosed as neurotics who were never hospitalized; Schizophrenics Anonymous, for ex-patients who were hospitalized with schizophrenia; and Alcoholics Anonymous, for those trying to overcome alcoholism and its related mental disorders.

Some discharged patients return to their homes, and these patients' families are able to start them on the road back into the world. Psychiatric social workers and visiting nurses may be called on to give the ex-patient's family the guidance and emotional support that they need. Home care seems to be most successful when the family members are nonjudgmental and are able to recognize the patient's limitations as well as strengths and abilities.

In two Missouri towns, former long-term mental patients were placed with foster-care families. Many of the patients improved so greatly that they were able to go on to lead completely independent lives. The key to their successful adjustment was found in the loving-kindness they received and their acceptance by the foster families and by the community as well.

A woman named Trudy, who was recently discharged from the Rochester Psychiatric Center in Rochester, New York, is benefiting from another kind of program, called Compeer (a rarely used word that means "companion" or "peer"). The Compeer program matches community volunteers with ex-mental patients on a one-to-one basis. When Trudy was discharged, Compeer put her in touch with Lisa, a University of Rochester graduate student who acted as her friend for one year. Together they did many things, from casually conversing over coffee to shopping for furniture. Now Trudy is living on her own and attributes her marvelous adjustment to the Compeer program and to Lisa.

Started in Rochester five years ago, the Compeer program is spreading through the state of New York. The coordinator of community education at Pilgrim Psychiatric Center in Suffolk, New York, is planning to start a Compeer program. "It will help with community attitudes and feelings that are so important for people to gain acceptance," she said.

Some Results of Deinstitutionalization

Despite the advances in treatment of the mentally ill, in society's thinking about the proper place for mental patients, and in the legislation meant to bring about change, the results have not been too good.

Communities complain that they are not prepared for the large numbers of patients who are deinstitutionalized. The policy, they hold, may have gone too far, too fast. Often, patients have found that they were not well enough prepared for living in the community. The fact that two out of every three discharged mental patients are returned to mental hospitals after release would seem to show that the policy is not working. A panel reporting to the president stated that deinstitutionalization "often aggravated the problem of the chronically mentally disabled."

Statistics also point to a lamentable drift towards transinstitutionalization of the mentally ill, especially among the elderly. Instead of being institutionalized in mental hospitals or living in community residences, many are now confined to nursing homes. It is estimated that about 75 percent of the men and women over sixty-five years of age now in nursing homes have mental disorders.

Jails, too, are being used to get ex-patients off the street. In Santa Clara, California, it is believed that about 10 percent of the mentally ill are incarcerated in prisons simply because they have no other care available to them. Sometimes they must wait a month or more in jail before they are readmitted to a hospital. Frequently, these victims of the system spend more time in jail than convicted criminals!

The problems with deinstitutionalization are so overwhelming that states that once welcomed the policy are beginning to reconsider their position. Some are slowing down the numbers of mental patients released from hospitals into the communities. The current rate is 3.6 percent as compared to 8 percent only a couple of years ago.

A number of lawsuits in California alleging that community facilities are understaffed and underfinanced has led some counties in the state to divert a number of patients from community programs back to state hospitals.

The daily newspapers carry more bad tidings of widespread dissatisfaction. In Colorado, the head of the State Division of Mental Health resigned after saying: "What we have done in the name of good mental health is to create a public tragedy. We have sent them [mental patients] from the back wards of Pueblo to the back alleys of Denver. It is a sin and a crime." And Dr. Eugene Feigelson, chief of psychiatry at New York's Downstate Medical Center, made a statement that put it this way: "We've done a lot of people a disservice to take away the supports that even a bad institution provided."

Most people who favor deinstitutionalization attribute its failure to two major problems. The first is a shortage of money, which limits attempts to provide good services for the released patients. Somehow the dollars allocated for patient care have not followed the ex-patients into the community. There are simply too few halfway houses and insufficient numbers of programs providing counseling, therapy, and aftercare to ex-patients.

Second, they blame the public, who still regard the mentally ill with apathy on the one hand, and fear and hostility on the other. Mental health and legal experts have proven over and over again that society is not threatened by releasing mental patients. The widespread and popular idea that the mentally ill are violent and dangerous is not supported by research evidence. As Dr. Shervert Frazier, Psychiatrist in Chief, McLean Hospital in Belmont, Massachusetts, said,

"Even among mental hospital patients, 98 to 99 percent are not dangerous. In states that have regulations and organized programs there are no grounds for fearing a halfway house in the neighborhood."

Although the results are disappointing, many advances have resulted from the milestone legislation that mandated deinstitutionalization. Some very successful programs show that the severely mentally ill can live and do well in the community when provided with sufficient funding and adequate services.

As a step in the right direction, New York City initiated the Community Support Systems project in 1979, to improve the services for the mentally ill. It grants funds for programs to provide aftercare for discharged mental patients and puts them in touch with the various government and voluntary agencies that can help ex-patients adjust to life outside institutions.

Ultimately, the outlook for the mentally ill in our society may depend not on the work of psychiatrists and social workers but on the action of the legislators, city planners, and the rest of society. What is needed is a redoubling of the effort to establish community-based mental health systems of the highest quality. With adequate funding, proper facilities and programs, the availability of therapy and education, and increased money for research, the discharged mental patients may finally get the chance they seek to take their rightful places as contributing members of the community.

Rights of Mental Patients

Over the last thirty years there has been an increased concern for the rights of women, minorities, and other disadvantaged groups. Within the last few years there has also been added a new and growing interest in protecting the rights of the mentally ill. Concern over these rights centers around a few basic questions: How much power should psychiatrists have over the lives of their patients? Can the state hospitalize patients against their will, and if so, under what circumstances? Do patients have the right to refuse treatment? Can hospitalized patients expect either to be treated or to be released?

Two groups that often find themselves on different sides of these questions are the mental health professionals and the safeguarders of civil liberties. Many medical authorities believe that only psychiatrists can adequately understand and deal with the complex problems of mental illness, and, therefore, they should be allowed to determine what is best for the patients and the people around them. Advocates of patients' rights, however, say that among the rights guaranteed by the United States Constitution is each person's freedom to make decisions about his or her own health. Further, where there is disagreement, the matter should be brought to an impartial court for a ruling.

These two views, the medical and the legal, are important in defining the rights of those who suffer the symptoms of mental illness.

Commitment and Release

The all-important decisions about who shall be committed to a mental institution and who shall be released is almost always made on the basis of a recommendation by one or more psychiatrists. Psychiatrists are also called on to determine the competency to stand trial of a person accused of a crime. They can recommend commitment of drug addicts and alcoholics to treatment programs. They can decide whether to institutionalize children in special schools.

One recent experiment points up the fallibility of psychiatrists in admitting patients to institutions. Twelve people not suffering from mental illness volunteered to present themselves to mental hospitals. They were instructed to act usual in all respects, with the exception of saying, falsely, that they heard voices. All twelve subjects were admitted by the psychiatrists who interviewed them. Eleven were diagnosed as schizophrenics, one as a manic-depressive. They were kept in the hospitals for periods of between seven and fifty-two days and in the course of their treatments were prescribed a total of 2,100 pills.

After they were released, the experimenter made his deception public. He also promised to repeat his experiment. Although he did not actually send any more people to the hospitals, the admitting staffs became much more cautious. Of the next 193 patients to be admitted, a hospital psychiatrist declared more than half of them pretenders. The person who conducted the study later wrote: "Any diagnostic process that lends itself so readily to massive errors of this sort cannot be a very reliable one."

Most patients who are placed in mental hospitals are so-called voluntary admissions. That is, they present themselves at the hospital of their own free will and ask to be accepted. Psychiatrists diagnose their conditions and decide whether or not they need to be hospitalized. Typically, such patients are kept from three to twenty days, with an average stay of about two weeks. Legally, they may leave whenever they want, but most states insist on a waiting period that may range from a number of hours up to thirty days.

Recently a young woman who voluntarily committed herself after her husband left her, found it was far easier to be admitted than to leave. For weeks, she struggled to convince the authorities that she was over her depression, but to no avail. Only after she got her family involved, and they hired a lawyer, was she finally discharged.

Every state also has a specific procedure for the involuntary commitment of individuals who give evidence of dangerous behavior to themselves or others. Usually this is done in court, with a judge deciding whether or not a person should be admitted. In most cases, though, the court appoints a psychiatrist to offer an opinion, and the judge goes along with the recommendation.

In many states, the patients who are the subjects of commitment hearings have few legal safeguards. They do not need to be notified that a hearing is taking place and do not need to be present. They are not entitled to testify nor to cross-examine the court-appointed psychiatrist. What's more, the individual who is threatened with involuntary commitment is not guaranteed the services of a lawyer, despite the fact that three times as many cases result in commitment without a lawyer as with. Even where counsel is provided by law, too few lawyers are both willing and able to represent clients effectively. And finally, the person has no assurance of a speedy hearing without extensive prehearing detention.

Those who approve of the present system believe that mental patients are incapable of recognizing their own condition. They argue that they are not competent to decide for or against hospitalization. Many believe that confinement of the mentally ill makes society safer. And, they point out, by focusing on patients' rights, we may overlook people who really need the care and treatment available at a hospital.

Opponents raise these questions: Should the court have the right to involuntarily commit someone on a suspicion that the person presents a danger to self or others? Is it enough for a psychiatrist to say, "In my opinion, this patient is dangerous," for the court to act? What about the elderly woman who is forgetful and sometimes leaves the oven on, creating a potential fire hazard? Or the model husband, father, and worker who goes on a drinking binge two or three times a year and on those occasions abuses his wife and children? Should these people spend a great deal of time in institutions?

Study after study shows that society is not made safer by isolating the mentally ill. In 1965 the National Committee on the Causes and Prevention of Violence issued a report saying that the discharged mentally ill, as a whole, are significantly less prone to violent behavior than the general population. Only 2.9 percent of ex-mental patients committed offenses that involved injury to another person. Yet, in spite of the rarity of violence among the mentally ill, many psychiatrists accept the concept of "preventive" detention.

Where there is a possibility of violent behavior, psychiatrists generally advise commitment, preferring to hospitalize ten "maybes" rather than allow one dangerous patient to be free. This practice, of course, runs counter to our system of justice, which puts the burden on the prosecution to prove that a person is guilty "beyond reasonable doubt" and would sooner let ten "maybes" go free rather than imprison one innocent man or woman.

Some psychiatrists try to preserve and extend their influence in determining "dangerousness" either for commitment or release. Judges are not qualified to make such decisions, they say, and legal commitment hearings delay treatment for those who need it and impede the proper practice of medicine.

A July 1974 task force report of the American Psychiatric Association cited a number of studies done on psychiatric accuracy in predicting violent or dangerous behavior in patients. In one California experiment a number of psychiatrists examined prisoners about to be released and overestimated the number considered to be potentially dangerous. Only 14 percent of those released were later arrested for a violent act or crime. Another project showed that the experts underestimated dangerousness and only correctly identified a risky individual one out of eight times. Some studies even found that ward attendants in mental hospitals are better at predicting dangerousness in the patients than are the trained psychiatrists.

The wrong judgment of two psychiatrists in the case of Adam Berwid is leading to new restrictions on the power of the professionals. Before his confinement in a New York State mental hospital, Berwid had attempted to kill his estranged wife. In the hospital, on several occasions, Berwid indicated that he was still intent on her murder. Nevertheless, in December 1979, the psychiatrists approved a furlough pass for Berwid, without informing either his former wife or the police. While on leave, Berwid stabbed and killed the woman.

The public was outraged and called for stricter controls on the release of mental patients from institutions. The New York State Office of Mental Health responded by drafting tough new rules that make it more difficult for psychiatrists to grant leaves for potentially dangerous patients. Now, a person considered dangerous must be cleared for a leave by a three-member panel of psychiatrists, not two as before, and must have the approval of an official of the Office of Mental Health. For discharge, the psychiatrist panel has to concur unanimously that the patient is no longer mentally ill, or that he or she "does not present an immediate threat to himself [or herself] or any other person."

In his book *The Powers of Psychiatry,* Dr. Jonas Robitscher, himself a psychiatrist, says that psychiatrists have some awesome powers that they have not shown much interest in curbing. Therefore, certain restraints are coming from outside the profession. "The infuriating quality of psychiatrists," Robitscher says, "is their insistence that they are scientific and correct." He has also written: "The psychiatrist would be a more acceptable and useful person, if he could more frequently bring himself to admit that there is the possibility that he is wrong."

Right of Privacy

Some psychiatrists, and patients too, view with concern a recent ruling in California that may be applied elsewhere. In the case of *Tarasoff* v. *Regents of the University of California,* a student in a university outpatient psychotherapy facility threatened to kill a former girl friend who had rejected him. Although the psychotherapist alerted the campus police, the university authorities countermanded the order. They said that putting the student under surveillance would violate his right to confidentiality. Later, the student did indeed kill the girl.

The girl's parents then sued the university, charging that they had failed to take steps to protect her life. The court ruled that a psychotherapist treating a mental patient does have a duty to try to avert any foreseeable danger arising from a patient's condition.

Critics of the ruling say it violates the patient's right to privacy in therapy. Dr. Alan Stone, a psychiatrist and a Harvard Law School professor, who is also the president of the American Psychiatric Association, believes that the decision will discourage difficult patients from seeking or continuing psychotherapy for fear of revealing a destructive side of themselves. He calls the ruling "highly disruptive of the patient-therapist relationship" and believes that it is not the best way to protect those who are threatened by dangerous patients. A survey of local psychiatrists and psychologists conducted in California by *The Stanford Law Review* shows that therapists believe patients will withhold information if they think that their therapists might breach confidentiality.

Supporters of the ruling, such as Professor Duncan Kennedy, also of the Harvard Law School, think that the *Tarasoff* court decision will not lessen the benefits for people who seek psychotherapy. He feels sure that therapists will continue their present practice of predicting the future conduct of their patients. Breach of confidentiality is nothing new. A substantial number of therapists warned about potentially dangerous patients even before the *Tarasoff* case.

The idea that an individual was under no obligation to control the conduct of another person and was not legally required to warn those who might suffer danger was a legal tradition that was followed for hundreds of years. The newer theory, that psychotherapists have a duty to warn the public, is a departure from this policy. The task now before the police, lawyers, and public officials is how to balance both of these rights—the patient's right to privacy and the public's right to be free of harm.

The Right to Treatment and
the Right to Refuse Treatment

In 1971 a landmark decision in the case of *Wyatt* v. *Stickney* established the right to treatment for all patients. Ricky Wyatt was a patient who had been involuntarily admitted to Bryce Hospital in Tuscaloosa, Alabama. An attorney, George Dean, found hospital conditions there to be very poor. The patients slept in large dormitories with no privacy, wore shoddy clothes, and were forced to do housekeeping for the hospital without pay. They were cared for by a poorly trained staff. Perhaps worst of all, there were so few psychotherapists at the hospital that Ricky and others like him did not receive any treatment.

Dean started a court case in the United States District Court on Ricky's behalf. The defendant was Dr. Stonewall Stickney, who was then the commissioner for mental health for Alabama. In his ruling, Judge Frank Johnson, Jr., said, "To deprive any citizen of his or her liberty upon the altruistic theory that the confinement is for humane therapeutic reasons and then fail to provide adequate treatment violates the very fundamentals of due process." The judge gave the state of Alabama six months to start treatment for all patients. Such treatment is defined as active treatment by qualified personnel in adequate numbers.

In actual fact, the requirements of Judge Johnson's orders went beyond the capabilities of the Alabama mental health system. The effect of this ruling was the release of large numbers of involuntarily committed patients. But the principle of right-to-treatment was established by this ruling and remains the basis of all involuntary hospitalizations.

Other court cases related to the right to treatment have established the principle that each patient be treated in the least restrictive environment. For some patients this means treatment as outpatients in community mental health centers or at some type of facility other than a mental hospital. Unfortunately, as discussed in the last chapter, the lack of funding and of proper facilities is slowing down the full realization of this decision.

In another prominent case, *O'Connor* v. *Donaldson*, fifty-three-year-old Donaldson sued officials of Chattahoochee State Hospital, Florida, for confining him for fourteen years without providing any treatment. Originally, his elderly, infirm parents reported that he suffered from delusions, and two doctors had committed Donaldson to the institution without even examining him. He succeeded in obtaining his freedom only after his twentieth petition for release was accepted for a hearing by a federal court.

More important than the award to Donaldson of damages amounting to $38,500 was that the case determined the principle of the right to freedom for mental patients. A patient who did not receive treatment could not be held in a hospital against his or her will. If there is no active treatment, the patient must be released.

In their 1975 opinion on this case, the Supreme Court asked, "May the State fence in the harmless mentally ill solely to save its citizens from exposure to those whose ways are different?" They decided that patients who are not dangerous and who are capable of surviving in freedom should be given their liberty.

As a result of the *O'Connor* v. *Donaldson* decision, too, a growing number of states are doing away with indeterminate involuntary commitment, which is confinement without a specific target date for discharge. Instead, they set a fixed period of time for hospitalization, after which the case is reviewed by psychiatrists, who either recommend continued hospitalization for another fixed period or else release the patient.

In some instances patients object to the treatment ordered for them as neither desirable nor necessary. Recent court decisions and laws are requiring signed notes of consent by patients or their guardians before any major treatment plan, such as ECT or psychosurgery, may be undertaken. This is giving patients the right to refuse treatment.

Until recently, there was no legal basis, except on religious grounds, for refusing drugs as part of treatment. Currently an organization called NAPA (Network Against Psychiatric Assault) is fighting for a patient's right not to be forced to take drugs. As one spokesperson put it, NAPA is opposed to "involuntary treatments for unwilling subjects."

Not long ago the press reported that a patient in a state

mental hospital, known only as Allen S., died after an attendant broke a bone in his neck while restraining him. Contributing to his death were confinement in a straitjacket for more than ten hours and forced feedings while sedated, restrained, and lying down.

Mechanical restraints such as straitjackets, chemical restraints such as drugs, as well as seclusion and isolation rooms, according to some former patients and staff members, are still used widely in mental hospitals. The director of one Pennsylvania hospital, for example, approved a form of "confrontation therapy," in which patients were forced by the use of cattle prods to face issues they had been avoiding. One patient who refused to bathe was regularly hosed and scrubbed with scouring powder.

By now, about half the states have laws regulating the use of restraints, mechanical or chemical. Attendants generally have to be authorized by hospital officials to use such devices. And limits are set on the length of time and frequency that such restraints may be used.

Patients who refuse treatment on the grounds that they are not sick present another thorny issue for psychiatrists and judges alike. If a patient is determined to commit suicide, for instance, the lack of treatment seems to go against the patient's most fundamental right—the right to life. With violent patients, there is the question of the rights of the staff and other patients to be free from assault by violent patients who refuse treatment.

Even disregarding the loss of liberty involved in compulsory treatment, it is not sufficiently clear that therapy given to an unwilling patient offers substantial benefit. A study reported in the *American Journal of Psychiatry* in 1974 showed what happened to a group of mental patients who left an institution in spite of medical advice not to do so. The results indicated that they fared as well as the control group, which remained in the hospital and received treatment there.

Doctors, judges, and patients sometimes find themselves as opponents rather than partners in their common goal of providing the best possible care and treatment for the mentally ill. What is needed is a joint effort to establish procedures that both protect the patient's basic civil liberties and meet his or her need for effective treatment. Further, there is a desperate need to raise standards in the mental hospitals and to implement the law regarding community-based services.

Rights of Children and Women

Often, children hospitalized for mental illness are in an even worse situation than adults. They may be deprived of their most fundamental rights to adequate care, treatment, and rehabilitation, as well as protection against physical and psychological abuse. Many are not aware of their legal rights and are victims of intimidation, harassment, and retaliation. Without access to or resources for counsel, children are frequently regarded as incompetent or too young to bring suit.

Children who are admitted to psychiatric institutions by their parents generally have neither the rights of voluntary patients nor the due-process protection given to involuntarily confined adults. Most citizens' groups that represent the interests of children lack the money and personnel to carry on the protracted and expensive lawsuits needed to right institutional wrongs.

Experts agree that the majority of children presently institutionalized could be treated in the community if sufficient programs existed. A federal court cited a study that showed that "more than half of Georgia's juvenile mental inpatients would not need hospitalization if other forms of care were available." In 1975, the Department of Health, Education and Welfare issued a report showing that only one-third of the children in St. Elizabeth's Hospital in Washington, D.C., and in twenty Texas mental institutions really needed to be in a hospital.

For centuries women have been in the unenviable position of being persuaded to enter mental hospitals or even railroaded into these institutions by manipulative husbands or fathers who objected to their behavior or wanted to be free of them. Ironically enough, one outstanding example is Mrs. E. T. W. Packard, an early advocate of mental patients' rights. Mrs. Packard was committed, in 1860, to an asylum by her husband. The reason was that she disagreed publicly with his views on religion. The law on the books at the time allowed husbands to commit their wives "without the evidence of insanity or distraction required in other cases." Inside the asylum she kept a secret account of asylum abuses. She described female asylum suicides as due to continual harassment, loneliness, and despair.

Today, more men and women are seeking psychiatric help than at any other time in history. Although statistics suggest that men outnumber women nearly 2 to 1 as patients in mental hospitals (see Table 4), women outnumber men as psychiatric outpatients by about 5 to 4. (See Table 5.)

Phyllis Chesler, in her book *Women and Madness,* says that women are often penalized by society for accepting female roles and acting depressed and anxious, as well as for rejecting traditional roles and acting hostile and aggressive. She cites many examples of women who were labeled mentally ill simply because they strayed from the narrow confines of what is considered "acceptable" behavior.

Female longevity, and a generally low regard for the elderly woman in our society, is held responsible for the fact that most patients over sixty-five in our psychiatric facilities are female. One major problem for elderly women is the lack of alternatives to confinement in hospitals, nursing homes, or other facilities. The scarcity of group homes for the disori-

Table 4.

Admissions to Inpatient
Psychiatric Services by
Age and Sex, United States, 1975 *

Sex and Age			
Male		Female	
Under 18	16,318	Under 18	8,934
18–24	52,323	18–24	19,518
25–34	67,530	25–34	33,331
35–44	39,637	35–44	25,472
45–54	41,147	45–54	24,735
55–64	19,469	55–64	16,624
65	12,513	65	8,046
TOTAL	248,937	TOTAL	136,300

Source: Department of Biometry and Epidemiology, NIMH.
* Last figures available

Table 5.

Admissions to Outpatient
Psychiatric Services by
Age and Sex, United States, 1975 *

Sex and Age			
Male		Female	
Under 18	227,411	Under 18	130,650
18–24	104,011	18–24	126,623
25–34	133,856	25–34	223,642
35–44	79,638	35–44	132,586
45–54	55,172	45–54	86,116
55–64	22,538	55–64	30,735
65	11,729	65	41,358
TOTAL	534,355	TOTAL	771,710

Source: Unpublished Data: Department of Biometry and Epidemiology, NIMH.
* Last figures available

ented woman, often without family and friends, means that she is faced with a choice between a mental institution and the terrors of the street. The tragedies that befall the "shopping bag ladies" in many of our cities are often due to the lack of community-based resources.

Women with young children who feel that they need residential treatment are frequently hesitant to enter a psychiatric facility. These patients want to preserve family ties and fear what will happen to their children while they are in treatment. The needs of both mothers and children in this situation require more thought than they have received.

According to Chesler, women seem to have a pattern of recurring hospital commitment and lengthier stays than their male counterparts. Perhaps this is due to the obstacles in the way of community-based care for women patients when they leave the hospital. Patients usually need some financial resources to support themselves. Many women have not worked before hospitalization and therefore do not have such means. Without money, they may be wholly dependent on "free" institutional care.

Some indicators also point out that women patients may be exposed to more radical therapies than men. One study found that three times as many women as men have been subjected to psychosurgery. A common therapy, the use of tranquilizing and mood-changing drugs, offers special problems for women, as some of these drugs upset the menstrual cycle and present unknown dangers for pregnant women. More research is needed on the side effects, long-term and short, of these drugs on women.

Among many other problems for institutionalized women is the danger of sexual attack from fellow patients and even from members of the staff. Women's quarters are often more confining and their liberties more restricted, "for their own protection." Occupational therapy and work available in the institutions seem to be confined to housekeeping, cleaning, and laundering. At best, a woman may receive beauty-operator training.

Ex-patients and civil rights advocates, among others, are working for reforms to strengthen women's rights in the mental health system. Stricter commitment standards and full-scale judicial hearings instead of admission by psychiatric certificate will give patients a chance to protest involuntary commitment. They will offer some protection against abuses by family members or commitment by psychiatrists who might be sexually biased in their thinking. Shortening the period allowed for "emergency" hospitalizations by relatives before a hearing is held and insisting on every woman's right to consult, at state expense if necessary, her own psychiatrist, will in the long run benefit both men and women.

Rights of Criminal Defendants

An ex-inmate of a psychiatric facility recently sued the state for involuntary commitment for thirty-four years. The man had been arrested forty years before for breaking into a railroad car and stealing six candy bars. Because he was found mentally incompetent to stand trial, the judge ordered him committed to an indefinite stay in the state mental hospital.

During the trial the defendant's lawyer pointed out that during his long confinement his client had not received any therapy, nor had he had any opportunity to prove his mental competency.

All people who are accused of crimes, under the American system of criminal justice, have the right to defend themselves in a court of law. In order to defend themselves, they must be capable of understanding the charges brought against them and be able to take an active part in presenting their side of the case. Defendants who are not able to understand the charges leveled against them, or who cannot help their lawyers defend them, are said to be "incompetent to stand trial."

In almost all cases, the judge, defense counsel, or prosecutor can request a competency evaluation for any defendant thought to be mentally disordered. Such requests are nearly always granted. The defendants are then sent to state mental hospitals for an evaluation, which may take up to three months. Although such defendants are almost always found to be competent, the practice persists. One 1972 study in Massachusetts showed that 95 percent of those committed for evaluation were indeed competent to stand trial.

Defendants that are found incompetent, though, without further hearing, are usually placed on indefinite commitment in a secure state hospital, or a prison mental hospital, as it is often called. The conditions here can be as bad as a prison or worse, with beatings, isolation, and all sorts of cruelty, including ECT and psychosurgery, used not as therapy but as punishment. Two recent cases involved the use of the chemical anectine, which causes choking, in the Vacaville facility in California (reported in the case of *Mackey* v. *Procunier*) and the use of apomorphine, responsible for a half-hour of vomiting, at the Iowa State Mental Facility (*Knecht* v. *Gillman*).

Unscrupulous prosecutors, according to Bruce Ennis and Richard Emery in their book, *The Rights of Mental Patients,* sometimes try to use the incompetency approach as a way of getting an individual locked up, without bail and without having to prove the case in court. Such defendants can "serve" more time in the prison mental hospitals than if there had been a trial and conviction and they had gone to jail.

Fighters for the rights of the mentally ill are now saying that defendants should not be sent for psychiatric evaluations over their objections, unless there is a full hearing to establish the probability of incompetency. Patients' rights advocates also want the evaluation to be done as quickly as possible and in the least restrictive environment. Then, if the person is found incompetent and is committed, there should be active treatment for a reasonable period of time. A person who is still not considered competent by the end of that period should be transferred to a noncriminal mental hospital and receive the same rights as all the other patients.

The insanity defense, which refers to the defendant's mental state at the time of the crime, is used far less often than the incompetence-to-stand-trial plea. The insanity defense is not often misused, since fewer than 1 percent of felony defendants invoke it and only a small percentage of those who make this plea are acquitted. Still, the controversy rages over whether it should be allowed at all and what the consequences should be for the defendant who is either judged to have been insane at the time of the crime or who is acquitted by reason of insanity.

A case that occurred several years ago illustrates the problems that sometimes result when people accused of crimes take a plea of insanity. A white policeman who shot and killed a black youngster who had insulted him was acquitted of the crime after the police officer's lawyer argued that the shooting took place when his client was temporarily insane. The jury deliberated and handed down a verdict of "not guilty by reason of insanity." Though the policeman was committed to a secure state mental hospital, he was discharged in less than two years, an act that angered many concerned members of the community.

An expert panel of scholars and lawyers recently concluded a study on the problems connected with the insanity defense. They proposed settling the issue by changing the wording of the insanity defense from "not guilty by reason of insanity" to "not responsible by reason of mental disease or defect." This change, they said, would better reflect a jury's conclusion that a defendant did indeed commit a crime, but that there should be different legal consequences due to that person's mental condition at the time.

Others say that defendants acquitted by reason of insanity should be allowed hearings before a second judge or jury to decide on commitment to a mental hospital. A defendant who was insane at the time of the crime, but not dangerous at the time of acquittal, should have a right to a civil, not criminal, commitment.

At the Crossroads

Very slowly both the public and the country's lawmakers are becoming concerned about the rights of the mentally ill and former mental patients. They are paying more attention to the release of troubled persons from mental hospitals. They are learning that all too often patients receive only custodial care in institutions, and many should not have been confined in the first place.

In the courts the mentally ill are beginning to win their legal rights to adequate care in the least restrictive environment and to protection from violations of their dignity as human beings and citizens of the United States.

What is needed now is a greater willingness on the part of society to provide adequate and appropriate care and treatment for all those who fall into the wide spectrum of the mentally ill. All of us have to come to understand that the mentally ill are not "them" as opposed to "us." As the Bible puts it, "We are members of one another."

At this time we are at the crossroads in mental health care. We can either take the road that leads to more humane treatment and continued progress in achieving justice and full legal rights for people with mental disorders, or we can take the path that leads back to confinement, deprivation of rights, prejudice, and discrimination. Future generations will pass judgment on whether we chose the wiser course.

Bibliography

Arieti, Silvano. *Interpretation of Schizophrenia*. 2nd ed. New York: Basic Books, 1974.

Benziger, Barbara. *Speaking Out: Therapists and Patients—How They Cure and Cope with Mental Illness Today*. New York: Walker, 1976.

Berne, Eric. *A Layman's Guide to Psychiatry and Psychoanalysis*. New York: Simon and Schuster, 1975.

Bernheim, Kayla, and Lewine, Richard. *Schizophrenia: Symptoms, Causes, Treatments*. New York: W. W. Norton, 1979. Covers many aspects of schizophrenia. Helpful for families who care for a member who is schizophrenic.

Cammer, Leonard. *Up from Depression*. New York: Simon and Schuster, 1969. Psychiatrist writes about symptoms and treatment of depression.

Chamberlain, Judi. *On Our Own: Patient-Controlled Alternatives to the Mental Health System*. New York: Dutton, 1978.

Chesler, Phyllis. *Women and Madness*. New York: Doubleday, 1972. About women in the mental health system and the care and treatment they receive in private therapy and psychiatric facilities.

Chu, F. D., and Trotter, S. *The Madness Establishment: Ralph Nader's Study Group Report on the NIMH*. New York: Grossman Publishers, 1974. Critical evaluation of the government's National Institute of Mental Health.

Deutsch, Albert. *The Mentally Ill in America*. New York: Columbia University Press, 1949. Comprehensive treatment of the history of psychiatry.

Ennis, Bruce, and Emery, Richard. *The Rights of Mental Patients*. New York: Avon, 1978. An American Civil Liberties Union Handbook on rights under present law and how to protect those rights.

Foucault, Michal. *Madness and Civilization*. New York: Random House, 1973. Thorough survey of care and treatment through the ages of those considered mentally ill.

Fraiberg, Selma. *The Magic Years*. New York: Scribners, 1968. Psychoanalyst writes about emotional needs of young children and how to deal with them.

Ginott, Haim. *Between Parent and Child*. New York: Avon Books, 1965. Describes how parents and children can communicate more directly.

Ginott, Haim. *Between Parent and Teenager*. New York: Avon Books, 1973. Helps parents and teenagers handle day-to-day crises and conflicts.

Horwitz, Elinor. *Madness, Magic and Medicine*. New York: Lippincott, 1977. Detailed history of mental illness.

Jones, Ernest. *The Life and Work of Sigmund Freud*. New York: Basic Books, Vol. 1, 1953; Vol. 2, 1955; Vol. 3, 1957. Abbreviated edition, 1961. Readable account of Freud, his life and work.

Kiev, Ari. *Courage to Live*. New York: T. Y. Crowell, 1979. About depression and ways to deal with the disorder.

Liston, Robert. *Patients or Prisoners?* New York: Franklin Watts, 1976. Discusses mental institutions in the United States and problems with the way mental illness is treated in these institutions.

Norton, G. Ron. *Parenting*. Englewood Cliffs, N.J.: Prentice-

Hall, 1977. Discusses problems in bringing up children, with a section on how to get help for disturbed children.

Park, Clara Claiborne, with Shapiro, Leon, M.D. *You Are Not Alone*. Boston, Mass.: Little, Brown, 1976. Comprehensive guide to mental illness, advice on how to get professional help, information on methods of treatment, facts about legal rights, and arguments pro and con concerning different therapies.

Pines, Maya. *The Brain Changers: Scientists and the New Mind Control*. New York: Harcourt Brace Jovanovich, 1973. Scientific research and the issue of mind control.

Robitscher, Jonas. *The Powers of Psychiatry*. Boston: Houghton-Mifflin, 1980. Psychiatrist describes sometimes awesome power of members of his profession and suggests need to curb some of their authority.

Rosen, George. *Madness in Society*. Chicago: University of Chicago Press, 1968. Social history of mental illness through the centuries.

Snyder, Solomon. *Madness and the Brain*. New York: McGraw-Hill, 1975. Good account of schizophrenia and its biochemical aspects.

Szasz, Thomas. *The Manufacture of Madness*. New York: Harper and Row, 1970. Psychiatrist condemns involuntary commitment to mental institutions as a threat to individual liberty and the rights of a citizen.

Szasz, Thomas. *The Myth of Mental Illness*. New York: Dell, 1961. 2nd rev. ed., Harper and Row, 1974. Discusses his belief that the concept of mental illness is erroneous and misleading and is based on false and immoral practices in society.

Ullman, L. H., and Krasner, L., eds. *Case Studies in Behavior Modification*. New York: Holt, Rinehart and Winston, 1965.

Wing, Lorna. *Autistic Children: A Guide for Parents and Professionals*. New York: Brunner/Mazel, 1972. Informs adults about guiding children diagnosed as autistic.

Suggested Reading

Beers, Clifford. *A Mind That Found Itself.* Rev. ed. New York: Doubleday, 1948. An autobiography in which Beers describes his efforts to recover from mental illness.

Benziger, Barbara. *Prison of My Mind.* New York: Walker, 1969. Autobiographical account of a woman's mental breakdown and her struggles to regain her sanity.

Burgess, Anthony. *A Clockwork Orange.* New York: Norton, 1963. Fantasy on the future of modifying behavior through negative conditioning in order to stop outbreaks of violence.

Donaldson, Kenneth. *Insanity Inside Out.* New York: Crown Publishers, 1976. Tells the story of how author was confined against his will in a mental institution for fifteen years before his case was won in the courts.

Farmer, Francis. *Will There Really Be a Morning?* New York: Putnam, 1972. Autobiography of an alcoholic who spent a long time in a state mental hospital during World War II.

Gotkin, Janet and Paul. *Too Much Anger, Too Many Tears.* New York: Times Books, 1975. A personal account of individual's triumph over psychiatry.

Green, Hannah. *I Never Promised You a Rose Garden.* New York: Holt, Rinehart and Winston, 1964. A fictionalized account of a teenage girl's three years in a mental hospital.

Guest, Judith. *Ordinary People.* New York: Viking Press, 1976. A seventeen-year-old boy comes home after eight months in a mental institution, and he and his family deal with his readjustment.

Huxley, Aldous. *Devils of Loudun.* New York: Harper and Row, 1971. Describes an incident in seventeenth-century England when young nuns at a convent charged the *curé* with being bewitched.

Kaplan, Bert. *The Inner World of Mental Illness.* New York: Harper and Row, 1964. A series of first-person accounts of what it is like to suffer the symptoms of mental illness.

MacCracken, Mary. *A Circle of Children.* New York: Lippincott, 1973. Extraordinary account of therapy with disturbed youngsters.

Mitford, Nancy. *Zelda.* New York: Harper and Row, 1970. Biography of Zelda Fitzgerald, gifted writer and wife of F. Scott Fitzgerald who suffered the effects of mental illness and psychiatric confinement.

Park, Clara Claiborne. *The Siege.* Boston: Little, Brown, 1972. Parent's view of what it is like to live with and teach an autistic child.

Plath, Sylvia. *The Bell Jar.* New York: Harper and Row, 1971. A fictionalized account of the mental breakdown of a highly gifted poet.

Rubin, Theodore. *Jordi.* New York: Ballantine, 1962. A story about a psychotic child.

Rubin, Theodore. *Lisa and David.* New York: Ballantine, 1962. About two mentally ill teenagers and how they are able to help each other.

Vonnegut, Mark. *The Eden Express.* New York: Bantam, 1976. Autobiographical account of the author's bout with schizophrenia.

Ward, Mary Jane. *The Snake Pit*. New York: New American Library, Signet, 1973. Originally written in 1946, this book exposed the worst aspects of mental institutions at that time.

Wechsler, James. *In a Darkness*. New York: W. W. Norton, 1972. Tragic account of a schizophrenic boy who commits suicide.

Wilson, Louise. *This Stranger My Son*. New York: Putnam, 1968. A mother tells how her son developed schizophrenia in early childhood.

Supplementary Tables

**Number of Admissions and Percent Change
in Number to Mental Health Services
for People of All Ages and for People Under 18,
United States, 1971 and 1975**

Type of Service and Age of Admissions	Number of Admissions		% Change 1971–1975
	1971	1975	
All Services *—			
All Ages	2,407,487	3,355,708	39.4
Under 18	443,372	655,036	47.7
State & County Mental Hospital (Inpatient)—			
All Ages	407,640	385,237	−5.5
Under 18	26,352	25,252	−4.2

* Includes inpatient services of state and county mental hospitals and of private psychiatric hospitals, general hospital psychiatric inpatient units, all services of community mental health centers, and outpatient psychiatric services. Excluded are VA services and those of residential treatment centers for emotionally disturbed children.

Number of Admissions

Type of Service and Age of Admissions	1971	1975	% Change 1971–1975
Private Psych. Hospital (Inpatient)—			
All Ages	87,000	129,832	49.2
Under 18	6,420	15,426	140.3
General Hospital Psychiatric Inpatient Units—			
All Ages	519,926	515,537	−0.8
Under 18	44,135	42,690	−3.3
Community Mental Health Centers—			
All Ages	411,548	919,037	123.3
Under 18	113,082	213,607	88.9
Outpatient Psychiatric Services—			
All Ages	981,373	1,406,065	43.3
Under 18	253,383	358,061	41.3

Source: Department of Biometry and Epidemiology, NIMH, 1978.

Estimated Resident Patients
in State and County Mental Hospitals
by Primary Diagnosis and Age, 1975

Primary Diagnosis	All Ages	Under 9	10–19	20–34	35–64	Over 65
Schizophrenia	93,240	128	2,972	19,990	47,880	22,270
Depression	1,248	—	43	267	643	295
Organic Brain Syndrome	38,879	50	739	2,767	13,215	22,109
Other Psychoses	8,827	1	70	640	3,497	4,619
Neuroses and Personality Disorders	8,142	18	1,173	3,354	2,835	762
Childhood Behavior Disorders	3,783	380	3,266	123	14	—
Alcohol/Drug Addiction	8,610	—	428	2,620	5,076	486
Others	28,662	287	2,869	9,050	12,801	3,654
TOTAL	191,391	864	11,560	38,811	85,961	54,195

(Age in Years column span over Under 9, 10–19, 20–34, 35–64, Over 65)

Source: Division of Biometry and Epidemiology, NIMH, 1978.

Admissions in 1977 to State and County
Mental Hospitals and to
Community Mental Health Centers by Diagnosis

Primary Diagnosis	State & County Hospitals	CMHC
Schizophrenia	142,008	125,808
Depression	42,987	147,288
Organic Brain Syndrome	23,010	26,065
Other Psychoses	4,086	11,336
Neuroses and Personality Disorders	24,226	218,075
Childhood Behavior Disorders	10,593	145,309
Alcohol/Drug Addiction	113,125	163,669
Others	45,985	210,661
Total	406,020	1,048,211

Source: Division of Biometry and Epidemiology, NIMH, 1980.

For Further Information or Professional Help

Academy of Orthomolecular Psychiatry
1691 Northern Boulevard
Manhasset, NY 11030

American Academy of Child Psychiatry
1424 16th Street N.W.
Suite 201A
Washington, DC 20036

American Academy of Clinical Psychiatrists
Vine Street Clinic
Stuart Building
610 East Vine Street
Springfield, IL 62703

American Academy of Psychotherapists
6363 Roswell Road
Atlanta, GA 30328

American Association for Geriatric Psychiatry
230 North Michigan Avenue
Suite 2400
Chicago, IL 60601

American Association for Social Psychiatry
201 S. Livingston Avenue
Livingston, NJ 07039

American Association of Psychiatric Services for Children
1725 K Street N.W.
Washington, DC 20006

American Family Therapy Association
15 Bond Street
Great Neck, NY 11021

American Mental Health Foundation
2 East 86th Street
New York, NY 10028

American Psychiatric Association
1700 18th Street N.W.
Washington, DC 20009

American Psychoanalytic Association
1 East 57th Street
New York, NY 10022

American Psychotherapy Association
P. O. Box 2436
West Palm Beach, FL 33402

American Schizophrenia Association
Huxley Institute
1114 First Avenue
New York, NY 10021

Association for Advancement of Behavior Therapy
420 Lexington Avenue
New York, NY 10017

Association for Research in Nervous
    and Mental Disease
Mount Sinai School of Medicine
100th Street at 5th Avenue
New York, NY 10029

Canadian Schizophrenia Foundation
2231 Broad Street
Regina, SK
Canada S4P 1Y7

Family Service Association of America
44 East 23rd Street
New York, NY 10010

Foundation for Depression and Manic Depression
7 East 67th Street
New York, NY 10021

Institute on Hospital and Community Psychiatry
1700 18th Street N.W.
Washington, DC 20009

International Transactional Analysis Association
1772 Vallejo Street
San Francisco, CA 94123

Mental Health Association
National Headquarters
1800 North Kent Street
Rosslyn, VA 22209

Mental Health Materials Center
419 Park Avenue South
New York, NY 10016

Mental Health Research Foundation
72 Burroughs Place
Bloomfield, NJ 07003

National Association for Mental Health
250 West 57th Street
Room 1425
New York, NY 10019

National Association of Private Psychiatric Hospitals
1701 K Street N.W.
Suite 1205
Washington, DC 20006

National Council of Community Mental Health Centers
2233 Wisconsin Avenue N.W.
Suite 322
Washington, DC 20007

National Institute of Mental Health
5600 Fishers Lane
Rockville, MD 20857

Psychiatric Services Section
American Hospital Association
840 North Lake Shore Drive
Chicago, IL 60611

Public Affairs Committee
381 Park Avenue South
New York, NY 10016

U.S. Department of Health and Human Services
Alcohol, Drug Abuse, and Mental Health Administration
5600 Fishers Lane
Rockville, MD 20857

Advocacy and Self-Help Groups

Alcoholics Anonymous
468 Park Avenue South
New York, NY 10016

American Association for the Abolition of Involuntary
    Mental Hospitalization
35 East 85th Street
New York, NY 10028

American Bar Association
Commission on the Mentally Disabled
1800 M Street, N.W.
Washington, DC 20036

ANAWIM
Loyola House
2599 Harvard Road
Berkley, MI 48702

THE BRIDGE
325 West 85th Street
New York, NY 10024

Center for the Study of Legal Authority and
    Mental Patient Status
132 Evergreen Avenue
Hartford, CT 06105

Emotions Anonymous
P.O. Box 4245
St. Paul, MN 55104

International Committee
    Against Mental Illness
P.O. Box 898
Ansonia Station
1990 Broadway
New York, NY 10023

Mental Disability Legal
    Resource Center
c/o American Bar Association
1155 East 60th Street
Chicago, IL 60637

Mental Health Law Project
1220 19th Street, N.W.
Washington, DC 20036

Mental Patients Association
2146 Yew Street
Vancouver, British Columbia

Mental Patients Civil Liberties Project
37 South 20th Street
Suite 601
Philadelphia, PA 19103

Mental Patients' Liberation Front
230 Boyleston Street
Boston, MA 02116

National Alliance for the Mentally Ill
500 North Broadway
St. Louis, MO 63102

National Center for Informed Depressives
P.O. Box 640
Bronxville, NY 10708

National Center for Law
and the Handicapped
1235 North Eddy Street
South Bend, IN 46617

National Committee
Against Mental Illness
1101 17th Street, N.W.
Washington, DC 20036

National Committee on Patient Advocacy
1800 North Kent Street
Arlington, VA 22209

Network Against Psychiatric Assault
2150 Market Street
San Francisco, CA 94114

Pathways to Independence
P.O. Box 651
McLean, VA 22101

Project Release
130 West 72nd Street
New York, NY 10024

Recovery
116 South Michigan Avenue
Chicago, IL 60603

Rehabilitation International
432 Park Avenue South
New York, NY 10016

Rough Times
Box 89
West Somerville, MA 02144

Society to Conquer Mental Illness
1710 Foothill Drive
Salt Lake City, UT 84108

Women Against Psychiatric Assault
2150 Market Street
San Francisco, CA 94114

World Federation for Mental Health
2075 Westbrook Crescent
University of British Columbia
Vancouver, BC
Canada V6T 1WS

Publications by
Ex-Patient Organizations

Action Magazine
B 1104 Ross Towers
710 Lodi Street
Syracuse, NY 13203

In a Nutshell
Mental Patients Association
2146 Yew Street
Vancouver, BC
Canada

Madness Network News
Network Against Psychiatric Assault
P.O. Box 684
San Francisco, CA 94101

Silent No Longer
Project Release
202 Riverside Drive, Apt. 4E
New York, NY 10025

State and Mind
Radical Therapist, Inc.
P.O. Box 89
West Somerville, MA 02144

Welcome Back
3206 Prospect Avenue
Cleveland, OH 44115

Glossary

Acute schizophrenia Most prevalent form of schizophrenia; may strike suddenly and without warning. See *Schizophrenia.*

Adaptations Helpful changes that make us better able to function.

Addiction Strong physical or psychological need for some chemical substance or drug.

Adult home Living facility in the community for physically or mentally disabled adults.

Agoraphobia Fear of open places.

Alzheimer's disease Disease that damages or destroys brain cells, leaving the patient mentally helpless; believed to be the cause of about half of all cases diagnosed as senile dementia.

Antidepressants Drugs used to treat severe depression; also called energizers.

Anxiety A generalized fear, unease, or apprehension without an objective cause.

Arteriosclerosis Hardening of the arteries that can cut circulation of blood to the brain and thus lead to injury to brain cells.

Autism Mental disorder in which the patient is more concerned with self than with reality; autism in children produces some of the same symptoms as schizophrenia.

Battle fatigue Mental condition with symptoms that include sleeplessness, nightmares, anxiety, tremors, and loss of appetite; usually temporary.

Behavior   A person's actions and reactions.

Behavioral therapist   Someone who uses an approach to treatment based on altering the patient's behavioral patterns.

Behavior modification   A form of therapy that alters behavior according to the principles of learning theory, rewarding the desirable acts and providing unpleasant associations for the undesirable acts.

Biofeedback   A method of using electronic instruments to make information on body functions, including pulse, temperature, blood pressure, etc., available to an individual to help that person control various reactions.

Brain tumor   A growth of tissue within the brain.

Cancer   A disease characterized by an uncontrolled growth of cells in or on the body.

Claustrophobia   Fear of closed spaces, such as elevators or small rooms.

Clinical psychologist   Usually someone holding a doctoral degree in psychology who is able to offer psychotherapy.

Compulsion   A strong impulse to perform some act or behave in a manner contrary to one's will or better judgment.

Conflict   The clash between two or more drives within an individual's personality.

Coping   Facing up to a problem or difficulty and usually achieving some degree of success in its resolution.

Counseling   Helping someone, either by offering suggestions and advice or by encouraging the person to find his or her own solutions.

Deinstitutionalization   The concept of moving patients who do not require hospitalization out of large institutions and into community settings.

Delusion   A strongly held belief that has no basis in fact or reality and that is held despite evidence to the contrary.

Depressive disorder   Strong feelings of sadness and/or apathy that are persistent and that interfere with normal functioning. Depressive neurosis is the mild form; depressive psychosis is more severe.

Desensitization A technique used to reduce tension and anxiety and substitute feelings of relaxation.

Deviant behavior Patterns of behavior that differ from the generally accepted norms.

Diagnosis Process of identifying specific physical or mental disorders.

Disease A condition in an organ, part, structure, or system of the body that interferes with its normal functioning.

Drug therapy Treatment of mind or behavior disorders by means of drugs.

ECT A treatment of severe mental disorders in which an electric current is passed through a patient's head to induce a convulsive seizure.

Ego The part of the personality concerned with the reality of the situation.

Electroconvulsive shock therapy See *ECT*.

Encephalitis Viral disease that, if untreated, can damage the brain and result in serious and permanent mental disability.

Encounter group A group, under a trained leader, that aims to help members break down the defenses that prevent them from enjoying meaningful relationships with others.

Energizers See *Antidepressants*.

Erhard Seminars Training See *Est*.

Est Large group therapy in which physical deprivation leads to acceptance of doctrines that promote better relations with others.

Family therapy Treatment approach in which an entire family meets with a therapist to discuss and seek solutions to common difficulties; usually initiated to help one particularly troubled family member.

Free association Patients say whatever comes to mind during psychoanalysis as a way of revealing unconscious thoughts and emotions.

Genetic Related to heredity. Characteristics are passed from parent to offspring through genes.

Group therapy Psychotherapy that takes place when a single therapist works with a number of patients at the same time.

Halfway house Residence with special program to help discharged mental patients readjust to life in the community.

Hallucination An experience or perception that seems real but that has no basis in fact. Hallucinations may be heard, smelled, tasted, felt, or seen.

Hypnosis An artificially induced state resembling sleep; sometimes used by psychotherapists to help an individual recall forgotten incidents or situations or bring about a change in behavior.

Hypoglycemia A disorder characterized by low blood sugar that may lead to such symptoms as depression, anxiety, phobias, and irritability.

Id The theoretical part of one's personality that strives for immediate pleasure and satisfaction.

Involuntary commitment Confinement in a mental hospital in spite of the patient's objections.

Lay analyst Someone who treats patients by psychoanalysis but who is not a trained psychiatrist.

Lithium A chemical, or more particularly its salt, that is used to treat the wide mood swings of manic-depressive psychosis.

Major tranquilizers Psychoactive drugs that reduce anxiety and calm fears; used to treat severe psychotic disorders.

Manic-depressive psychosis A mental disorder characterized by wide mood swings from excitement and elation (mania) to sadness and apathy (depression).

Mental illness Any behavioral or psychological condition that causes the person stress and interferes to a lesser or greater extent with a person's ability to function on a day-to-day basis.

Mental retardation A condition that prevents a person from functioning on the same intellectual level as most others of the same age.

Milieu therapy   A treatment method that uses the environment to bring about changes in patient behavior.

Minor tranquilizers   Drugs used to reduce anxiety and tension in people with neurotic symptoms.

Narcotics   Any of a number of substances that produce feelings of euphoria, cause a stupor, or relieve pain.

Neurosis   A symptom or group of symptoms that is found unacceptable by the person and causes distress. The symptoms are enduring, have no organic basis, and are not grossly different from the norm.

Neurotic   A person with a neurosis. See *Neurosis.*

Normal   Standard, common, usual, average. Free from mental disorder.

Obsession   Persistent or recurrent ideas, thoughts, images, or impulses that are not under a person's voluntary control.

Occupational therapy   Easy tasks, such as basketry or simple carpentry, given to patients for diversion, for exercise, and to develop vocational skills.

Organic model   The view that all mental disorders stem from physical changes or damage within the body.

Organic therapies   The treatment methods that depend mostly on drugs, special diets, electroconvulsive shock, or psychosurgery to control or relieve the symptoms of severe mental disorders.

Orthomolecular psychiatry   A view that holds that mental disorders spring from improper balances of chemicals within the body or the brain.

Paranoid schizophrenia   The second most prevalent form of schizophrenia, characterized by sets of changeable delusions and hallucinations, which can lead to bizarre, unpredictable, and sometimes dangerous behavior.

Paresis   A mental condition that results from the disease syphilis.

Personality   An individual's behavior patterns, which include the way one relates to, perceives, and thinks about the environment and oneself.

Personality disorder   Any condition that interferes with the normal functioning of an individual's personality.

Phobia neurosis   A strong and persistent fear of an object, activity, or situation that actually presents much less danger than the reaction indicates.

Primal therapy   A group therapy approach that helps the patient free the emotions in a primal scream.

Projection   A defense mechanism in which a person denies a desirable or an undesirable trait in himself or herself and attributes (projects) it to others.

Psychiatric facility   An institution devoted to the care and treatment of mental patients.

Psychiatric nurse   A person with professional nursing education and training who specialized in the prevention, care, and treatment of mental illnesses.

Psychiatric social worker   Someone with advanced training in social work, with a specialty in psychiatry.

Psychiatrist   A medical doctor who specializes in the treatment of mental illnesses.

Psychoanalyst   A psychiatrist with special training in the use of psychoanalysis as a treatment method.

Psychodrama   One form of group therapy in which people act out troublesome incidents or feelings as a way of gaining insights into their own fears, behavior, and emotions.

Psychologist   A person who holds a degree in psychology—the study of the human mind and human behavior.

Psychosis   Loss of touch with reality; distortions in perception, behavior, thinking, emotions, and speech; the most severe type of mental disorder.

Psychosocial model   A view of mental illness that focuses on the role of the family and the surroundings on the individual.

Psychosurgery Brain surgery in which nerve pathways in the brain are cut in order to alter behavior; used only on severely psychotic patients.

Psychotherapies Treatment methods that use talk between the patient and therapist as the main means of uncovering the hidden sources of illness.

Psychotherapist A professionally trained individual who treats mental illness or personality disorders by psychological means.

Rehabilitation An effort to restore someone to a condition of good health and the ability to function as before.

Repression The forcing of shocking or painful images and memories out of one's conscious thoughts and into the unconscious.

Resistance A stage in psychoanalytic treatment in which the patient fights the process by getting angry with the analyst and blocking the flow of free association.

Restraints Mechanical means, such as straitjackets, or chemical means, such as tranquilizer drugs, that prevent patients from moving about freely.

Schizophrenia A severe, complex, psychotic disorder that affects all aspects of a sufferer's personality; includes bizarre behavior, delusions, hallucinations, and withdrawal into one's own thoughts and fantasies.

Senile dementia Symptoms of memory loss, disorientation of time and place, and impaired thinking ability, sometimes thought to be associated with old age.

Sensitivity training group A type of group therapy designed to help individuals overcome their distrust of others.

Societal reaction model A view that regards the symptoms of mental illness not as a disorder but as an adaptation of the individual to society.

Stimulants Drugs that speed up the functioning of the nervous system, increasing physical and mental activity.

Straitjacket A garment made of strong fabric used to bind the arms and subdue violent or dangerous mental patients.

Stress A situation in which the environment makes greater demands on a person than the individual feels able to meet.

Stroke A break in the wall of one of the blood vessels in the brain, which results in damage or destruction of brain cells and may impair mental functioning.

Superego The theoretical conscience, or ego-ideal part of the personality; mostly learned from parents.

Syphilis A disease caused by bacteria that, if untreated, can strike at the brain and leave the victim mentally disabled.

Tardive dyskinesia A disfiguring and disabling condition that results from long-term use of antipsychotic drugs.

Tension Mental or emotional strain or anxiety.

T group See *Sensitivity training group.*

Therapist Someone who is trained in the treatment of mental disorders.

Tranquilizers A number of drugs used to induce calmness and reduce tension. See *Major tranquilizers* and *Minor tranquilizers.*

Transactional therapy A patient is helped by this group therapy approach toward better interpersonal relations by understanding how all three parts of the personality work in social situations.

Transinstitutionalization The movement of patients from one institution to another, such as from a state hospital to a nursing home or a jail.

Voluntary admission The patient who asks to be placed in a mental hospital.

Index

Acute schizophrenia, 41, 42, 69, 70, 125
Adaptation, 15, 16, 125
Addiction, 56, 67–68, 69–70, 86, 125
Adler, Alfred, 32
Adult home, 76–78, 125
Alcohol abuse, 10, 15, 28, 45, 48, 51, 55–56, 81, 86, 88
Alcoholics Anonymous, 56, 81, 119
Alzheimer's disease, 52, 125
Antidepressant, 65–66, 125
Anxiety, 24, 25, 26, 27–28, 29, 33, 34, 55, 62, 64, 69, 71, 74, 125
Arteriosclerosis, 52, 125
Autism, 39, 125

Beer, Clifford, 6
Behavior, 13, 126
Behavioral theory, 33–34

Behavioral therapist, 126
Behavioral therapy, 62–65
Behaviorist, 33, 62–65
Behavior modification, 62–63, 126
Berwid, Adam, 89
Biochemical factors, 43, 44, 46, 48, 49, 52, 69
Biofeedback, 64, 126
Bleuler, Dr. Eugen, 40
Brain damage, 10, 51, 52, 53–55, 67, 71
Brain tumor, 54, 126

Children's rights, 95–98
Clinical psychologist, 20, 126
Combined treatment, 57
Community mental health center, 23, 74, 92
Community Mental Health Centers Act, 74
Compulsion, 30, 126

Confrontation therapy, 94
Criminal defendants' rights,
    99–102

Dangerousness, 83–84, 88,
    89, 91, 93
Deinstitutionalization, 8,
    74–76, 82, 83, 84, 126
Delusion, 16, 36–38, 40, 42,
    70, 126
Depression, 9, 16, 30, 31,
    54, 69, 70, 71, 87, 96
Depressive neurosis, 30–31,
    52, 127
Depressive psychosis, 65,
    127
Desensitization, 63–64
Drug abuse, 10, 15, 45, 48,
    51, 55–56, 69–70
Drug therapy, 43, 52–53,
    55, 57, 95, 98, 127
    side effects, 67, 68, 98

ECT, 57, 69, 70–71, 76, 93,
    127
Elderly, 51, 67, 82, 88, 96,
    97
Electroshock. See ECT
Emotional blunting, 39, 53
Encephalitis, 51, 53, 127
Encounter group, 60, 127
Environmental factors, 10–
    11, 13, 45, 46, 48, 49,
    61–62
est, 61, 127

Family therapy, 61, 127
Foster care, 81
Free association, 57–58,
    127
Freud, Sigmund, 6, 26, 29,
    31, 32, 33, 57

Genetic factors, 13, 44, 45,
    48, 69–70, 128
Group therapy, 59, 61, 65,
    128

Halfway house, 78–80, 83,
    128
Hallucination, 16, 36–38,
    42, 55, 56, 65, 70, 128
Heroin, 56, 69, 70
Home care, 81
Hypnosis, 59, 128
Hypoglycemia, 69, 128

Incompetency, 99, 100, 101
Insanity defense, 101
Involuntary commitment,
    87, 91, 92, 93, 99, 128

Jung, Carl, 32, 33

Knecht v. Gillman, 100

Laing, R. D., 11–12
Lay analysis, 20, 128
Lithium, 66, 128

Mackey v. Procunier, 100

Manic-depressive psychosis, 47, 66, 86, 128
Marijuana, 56, 69
Mental health, 12–16, 20, 21, 34, 80
Mental illness
aftercare and rehabilitation, 19, 72–84, 131
causes, 1, 2, 3, 7, 10–12
See also Biochemical factors, Environmental factors, Genetic factors, Personality factors
classification, 1, 9–10
definition, 9–10, 128
history, 1–8
incidence, 16–19, 51
legal aspects. *See* Children's rights, Criminal defendants' rights, *Mackey* v. *Procunier, O'Connor* v. *Donaldson,* Right of privacy, Right to treatment, *Tarasoff* v. *Regents of the U. of California,* Women's rights, *Wyatt* v. *Stickney*
prevention, 12–16, 19. *See also* Mental health
research, 7–9, 10
symptoms, 6, 22. *See also* Anxiety, Compulsion, Delusion, Depression, Hallucination, Obsession
Mental institutions, 4, 5, 6, 7, 8, 18, 20, 73, 86, 96, 97, 98
Mental retardation, 8, 73, 128–129
Milieu therapy, 61–62

Narcotics, 56, 129
National Institute of Mental Health, 46, 50, 52, 118
Network Against Psychiatric Assault, 93, 121
Neurosis, 25–34, 58, 129
Neurotic, 25, 26, 27, 28, 30, 31, 32, 33, 34, 60, 62, 65, 66, 81, 129
Nursing home, 82

Obsession, 30, 129
O'Connor v. *Donaldson,* 92–93
Organic model, 10, 129
Organic therapy, 57
Orthomolecular psychiatry, 69–70, 129

Paranoid schizophrenia, 41–42, 129
Patients' rights, 85–102
Personality factors, 13, 14–16, 31, 32, 33, 34, 40, 46, 50, 57, 60–61, 130
Phobia neurosis, 28, 63–64, 69, 71, 130
Primal therapy, 60, 130
Psychiatric nurse, 19, 72, 130

Psychiatric social worker, 20, 61, 78, 81, 130

Psychiatrist, 19, 20, 31, 34, 38, 39, 40–43, 47, 58, 67, 71, 73, 84–86, 87–91, 99, 130

Psychoanalysis, 20, 31–34, 57, 58

Psychoanalyst, 19, 57, 130

Psychodrama, 59–60, 130

Psychologist, 20, 34, 91, 130

Psychosis, 35–50, 58, 130

Psychosocial model, 11, 130

Psychosurgery, 57, 71–72, 93, 98, 100, 131

Psychotherapist, 20, 131

Psychotherapy, 57–64

Psychotic, 35, 77

Revolving door patient, 78

Right of privacy, 90–91

Right to treatment, 91–95

Schizophrenia, 16, 39–46, 48, 50, 67, 69, 76, 81, 86, 131

Self-help group, 80–82

Senile dementia, 18, 51–53, 131

Senility. See Senile dementia

Sensitivity training group, 60, 131

Short-term, Anxiety-provoking Psychotherapy, 59

Societal reaction model, 11, 131

Stress, 13, 15, 16, 22, 27, 43, 48, 70, 132

Stroke, 10, 52, 132

Suicide, 18, 23, 31, 46, 47, 48, 49, 50, 70, 72, 94, 96

Syphilis, 10, 51, 53, 132

Tarasoff v. Regents of the U. of California, 90, 91

Tardive dyskinesia, 67

Therapist, 20, 132

Thought disorders, 38–39, 40, 51, 65, 68

Tranquilizers, 7, 16, 132
  major, 65, 128
  minor, 66, 129

Transactional therapy, 60–61, 132

Transinstitutionalization, 82, 132

Treatment, 2, 3, 4, 7, 8, 16, 18, 19, 22–24, 32–34, 38, 41, 43, 55, 57–72, 73, 92. See also specific treatments

Violence, 83–84

Voluntary admission, 87, 132

Witches, 3, 4, 11

Women, 3, 8, 27, 67

Women's rights, 95–98

Wyatt v. Stickney, 91